Roger L Brooks

THE POWER OF
LOYALTY™

10 Essential Steps
TO BUILD A SUCCESSFUL
CUSTOMER LOYALTY STRATEGY

E_P
Entrepreneur.
Press

Published by ENTREPRENEUR PRESS®
Permission to reproduce or transmit any of the material contained within this
book must be obtained in writing from the author.

The Power of Loyalty™ is a registered trademark of Roger L. Brooks.
To order additional copies of this book call (866) 498-9248.

Additional inquiries can be directed to:
Roger L. Brooks, Inc.
PO Box 2689
Binghamton, NY 13902
Phone (607) 584-5109
E-mail: info@thepowerofloyalty.com
Website: thepowerofloyalty.com

Cover design by: Elsan Dzudza
Contributing editor: Nancy Blanford
Production and composition: Eliot House Productions
Photography by: Ed Aswad

First Printing: May 2010

Library of Congress Cataloging-in-Publication Data
    Brooks, Roger L.
    The power of loyalty/by Roger L. Brooks.
        p. cm.
        ISBN-13: 978-1-59918-393-0 (alk. paper)
        ISBN-10: 1-59918-393-5
        1. Customer loyalty. 2. Customer relations. 3. Marketing research. I. Title.
    HF5415.525.B76 2010
    658.8'343—dc22   2010006662

Printed in Canada

14 13 12 11 10   1 2 3 4 5 6 7 8 9 10

Loyal Dedication

AFTER BOARDING AN AIRPLANE WHILE on a business trip in the summer of 2007, my brother-in-law, Ray Stanton, handed me a book to read. It was Jeffrey Gitomer's *Little Red Book of Selling.* As a salesman, I couldn't get enough of the book. I began making immediate changes in my approach because I had a whole new outlook on why customers want to buy. Reading the book was also the beginning of a new chapter in my life. Gitomer's words helped me open my eyes to my true passion in life and what I love to do most—WRITE.

I dedicate this book to two very important people, as this publication would not have been possible without them:

- Ray Stanton III. For introducing me to *Little Red Book of Selling*, and for providing me with opportunity my entire professional career. I learned about The Power of Loyalty from Ray Stanton. Ray, I am deeply grateful for all that you do.
- Jeffrey Gitomer. For helping me to get underneath the surface of myself. I am appreciative of your candor and how much you have contributed to improving the lives of salespeople everywhere. Although each word in this book is based on my own thoughts and experiences, I've adopted your teachings and molded them into my own style. Thank you for sharing sales secrets that have helped change the lives of salespeople around the globe. I will strive to follow suit by helping those who want to implement or enhance their customer loyalty strategies. Thank you, Jeffrey!

"Give your customers a REASON to be LOYAL, because if you DON'T, your competition WILL!"

—Roger L. Brooks

Contents

Loyalty Profiles

Dedication and Acknowledgments

I WOULD LIKE TO PAY A SPECIAL TRIBUTE to the publishing team at Entrepreneur Media. Publisher Jere Calmes, director of marketing Leanne Harvey, marketing specialist Jillian McTigue, corporate counsel Ron Young, and production coordinator Karen Billipp.

I also want to thank those who have played an important role in my life. They have all been loyal to me, and I am loyal and grateful to each of them in return. Thank you all!

My lifelong friend and cousin A. J. Stillittano. My very close friends Mike Hrehor, Freddy Seymour, Tony Brunelli, Jon Myers, Matt Kennedy, and Anthony Capozzi. A special thank you to Mirko Gojkovic. Thanks for all of the healthy debates and brainstorming about *our world* of loyalty.

Some other people who have played an important part in my life are Coach Fran Heath, Tim Lee, Nick Cannon, Mark Vinci, Mike Carboni, King Rice, Al Trager, Glenn McIver, Tim Mollen, Marty Burnett, Matt Regulski, Billy Berg, Matt Fiato, Scott Spagnolli, Scott Mullins, Jeffrey Levine, Albert Diluzio, Rev. Joe Salerno, Stephen Smyk, Jud Blanchard, Pat Maughan, Dr. John Perry, Juanita M. Crabb, Rev. Amedeo Guida, Mark Yonaty, Coach Jack Dunn, Marlon Waren, Jim Flad, Jim Sapp, Clyde Drexler, Ray and Nikki Stanton, Luke Stanton, Tom Stanton, Ken Heinrich, Art Christensen, Jackie Gow, Shannon Mess, Anna Acquisto, Jim Orband, Ken Tomko, Jim Franz, Su Jung Ah, Dan Farrell, Mirko Gojkovic, Tricia Farrant, Dragosalv Bogicevic, David Schachne, Senator Tom Libous,

Don Puglisi, Fran and Helen Battisti, Bill Dexheimer, Lloyd Ketchum, Albert Nocciolino, Mike Tasevski, Stacie Broadway, Ed Aswad, Dennis Driscoll, Todd Thompson, John Rumpel, Natalie Knudson, Uncle Tony Milasi, Uncle Rodney Brooks, Paul Fiacco, Donna Bryan, Aunt Angie Donovan, Bob Vallone, Buster Fiacco, Jim Rotella, Jim Vallone, Marty Tassoni, and Michal Slaby.

A very special thank you to my Aunt Mildred Brooks who always encouraged me to write.

TO MY IMMEDIATE FAMILY: My wonderful and kind sister and brother-in-law, Stephanie and Steve Pirozzi. My parents, Roger and Nancy Brooks, and their unconditional love and support. My mother- and father-in-law, Rosetta and Sergi DeRitis. Special cousin Thomas Montefusco. My sister-in-law, Romina Stanton. My nieces and nephews: Raymie, Gabby, Julia, and Max Stanton and Sophia and Maia Pirozzi. My children Alexis and Roger II. You two are my biggest accomplishment in life!

TO MY QUEEN: My wife, my best friend, confidante, and soulmate. Thank you from the *bottom* of my heart for your constant support, encouragement, and sacrifice. This book would not have been possible without you, Sabrina, and I will be forever *loyal* to you.

LOYALTY

Who is the most loyal person you know?

What companies are you most loyal to?

What brands are you most loyal to?

Are your family members loyal?

Are your co-workers loyal?

Who is most loyal to you?

Is your spouse loyal?

Is your pet loyal?

Are you loyal?

Why are these trivial questions so important? Because in order to understand loyalty, customer loyalty, the substance behind loyalty strategies, and *The Power of Loyalty*, it's important to understand the vital part loyalty plays in the lives of your customers and how it has the potential to change their behavior so they become more profitable.

There will always be naysayers criticizing the effectiveness of loyalty, loyalty programs, and loyalty strategies. However, if you take the time to treat your customers well and reward them for their behavior, only good things can stem from that. In essence, that is where loyalty begins.

If I had my way, every elementary school in America would teach children the importance and significance of loyalty. Teaching children the importance of loyalty would promote better character.

Promoting loyalty breeds:

Trustworthiness
Dependability
Allegiance
Devotion
Excellence!

The Power of Loyalty will plunge into the substance behind the word loyalty. It will provide an understanding of how loyalty can change your perspective in day-to-day thinking and give you an inside view of the overall customer loyalty experience. In addition, the book will guide you through the essential steps to building a successful loyalty strategy.

Want to receive ongoing tips and information regarding loyalty strategies?

Go to

thepowerofloyalty.com/tips

Provide your name and e-mail address, and I'll send you periodic updates!

Preface

I CAN REACH BACK AND REMEMBER each detail. It was my first Starbucks experience. The year was 1990, and I had recently moved to Portland, Oregon, from upstate New York to attend Portland State University. I was a 20-year-old junior college transfer trying to walk on to the Division I Portland State University Vikings baseball team led by Coach Jack Dunn.

I made some friends within the first couple days of tryouts, and after the third day a few of the guys asked if I wanted to join them to "grab a coffee." I'll admit, I thought the request was some sort of code name to go out and "grab a beer." I accepted, and five of us walked down the city park blocks, just past Nordstrom, and went into a small standalone building called *Starbucks Coffee*. Each of my teammates stood in line and in some sort of coffee cult-like language placed an order. I remember looking at the large display menu behind the counter, but I wasn't sure what I was reading. There were foreign words displayed on the menu such as "Cappuccino," "Latte," and "Mocha."

Three of my teammates quickly ordered in foreign tongues, and I recall feeling nervous as the time came closer for me to order. "I'll have a tall, nonfat, no-whip mocha," the teammate in front of me ordered. "I'll have the same," I said (although I had no idea what I just ordered). This was the first cup of coffee I had ordered in my entire life. The closest thing I'd had to a cup of coffee was the coffee-flavored hard candy my mother bought when we were kids (routinely the last type of candy left in our house).

After waiting a few minutes for my $3 "tall, nonfat, no-whip mocha," I joined my teammates who were sitting on bar stools at a tall table near the window facing S.W. Broadway.

I remember looking around thinking, "This is really different but this is very neat." It was a whole new experience; and the atmosphere, the aroma, and my first Starbucks coffee are things I will never forget. That was my introduction to coffee, it was my introduction to Starbucks, and what I wouldn't realize until years later—my introduction to customer loyalty.

I did find the experience somewhat odd for 20-something college baseball players. But I took notice. At least in Portland, Oregon, in 1990 I was witnessing and living a culture change. I was exposed to the coffee revolution firsthand, and I knew it would have an impact not only in Portland but also much further beyond. I knew I couldn't wait to go back to Starbucks again.

Little did I know that I would visit hundreds of Starbucks in dozens of cities throughout North America in the years to come; and little did I know that my first Starbucks experience would be replicated, almost identically, each and every visit.

A few weeks later, Coach Dunn sat me down in his office to give me the bad news. For the first time in my life I had to admit to myself that I wouldn't play baseball at the highest collegiate level. I also had to admit that I wouldn't come close to playing baseball as a career. All the hard work and all of my childhood dreams came to an end that day—until Coach Dunn shared some advice that I would remember and cherish forever.

"I've been coaching baseball for more than 35 years," he said. "In all my years of coaching and the hundreds of talented kids that went through the system, there were only three players I coached who made it to the big leagues—Jeff Lahti, Steve Olin, and Dale Murphy. Roger, we all have talents. Find your special talent and you will find happiness. Be loyal, and loyalty will be returned to you tenfold. It's a law of life."

That was the last day I put on a glove and threw a ball playing organized baseball, but my coach's words would resonate in my mind for years to come. The experience at Starbucks and my separation from baseball were the foundation, my introduction to loyalty. I'm very grateful for that.

"Be loyal, and loyalty will be returned to you tenfold. It's a law of life."

—Coach Jack Dunn,
Portland State University, Vikings Baseball

I'm sure you can remember the first time you walked into a Starbucks Coffee. The reason you remember it is because the braintrust at Starbucks planned it that way. They wanted to make certain there would be a lasting impact from your first visit, and wanted to make sure you had a memorable first impression so you couldn't wait to come back again to buy. And it worked. You went back again, and again, and again. And you told your friends, and they told their friends.

Each time you went back, chances are you had a good experience. You enjoyed the coffee, you enjoyed the aroma, you enjoyed the atmosphere, and you enjoyed the music. Most likely, and most importantly, you were satisfied with the level of service you received from the barista preparing your coffee behind the counter. The barista was funny, friendly, and uplifting in a manner that you were not used to seeing or being treated by any other "everyday" establishment. More than likely, you were satisfied with the overall experience.

The more you frequent Starbucks the more you realize that the barista doesn't only treat you the way she did, rather she treats each and every customer the same way. That consistency is a key ingredient that contributes to Starbucks' success. The loyal customer base Starbucks has built over the years is one of the most successful in the history of modern food service. Starbucks *literally* gets people hooked.

So just how does Starbucks do it and why don't others follow? Answer: because it's not easily replicated. The Starbucks experience cannot be replicated without a strong financial commitment and a major change in corporate culture. It wasn't by chance that all the pieces came together on your first, fifth, and fiftieth visit to Starbucks.

It was an extremely well-thought-out strategy to persuade customers to be loyal to Starbucks and to the brand from the very first time they set foot in one of its coffee houses. Starbucks aims to connect to *multiple senses* of each customer—in such a way that the customer craves to repeat the experience. Of course, Starbucks has mastered its main product, its coffee, yet it has also mastered the experience. It is the added perks you receive that give you a *consumer thirst* to want to go back again and again. As much as coffee is addictive, the experience becomes equally addictive.

If you haven't read it already, I recommend *The Starbucks Experience* by Joseph A. Michelli, Ph.D. You will learn every detail of why Starbucks is the number-one coffee retailer in the world. You will learn why it is an expert in food service retailing and how it has been able to continue to prosper year after year. It has an exclusive approach to everything it does from how it trains and treats its employees to how it selects the coffee beans it brews.

In July 2008, Starbucks closed approximately 600 underperforming stores in an effort to ease its financial woes. It has been reported that the reasons it closed nearly 10 percent of its shops in the U.S. were the weakening economy, fierce competition, and cannibalization from its own stores.

As much as coffee is addictive, the experience becomes equally addictive.

More recently, Starbucks initiated a customer loyalty program, My Starbucks Rewards, and the timing couldn't have been better. The rewards program will be a key driver to fighting competing businesses such as Dunkin' Donuts and McDonald's, as well as emerging competition from hometown coffee houses. The program strategy for My Starbucks Rewards will be one of the most important decisions Starbucks has made for its company's future. Due to the size and scale of the program, Starbucks must find a way to wow its customers with an exciting program offering attractive benefits.

Currently, there are three levels to the Starbucks program: WELCOME LEVEL, GREEN LEVEL, and GOLD LEVEL. Each level has its own set of benefits, and members can graduate to the next level by making ongoing purchases. You can receive additional details on the program by visiting starbucks.com/card.

There are dozens of examples like Starbucks out there. My goal is to provide you thought-provoking insights on the importance of customer loyalty, customer loyalty programs, and customer loyalty strategies.

If you are a small-business owner, entrepreneur, or corporate executive researching options for a new program or you work for a company that has an existing customer loyalty program you're looking to enhance, I'm confident you'll receive information here that will assist you and/or complement your current efforts.

Administering a customer loyalty strategy demands a great deal of time, attention, thought, effort, sweat and tears, but there are few books written about the fundamentals of launching or enhancing customer loyalty strategies. My objective is to provide you with insights and value that will save you time and money in the end.

I intend to take all the knowledge and experience I have on loyalty strategies and publish that knowledge indefinitely for my readership in the form of weekly e-mails, news articles, trade publications, and books. *The Power of Loyalty* is the first book of its kind on the subject of loyalty, but rest assured, it will not be the last book I write on this topic. There's much to cover on loyalty. In this first book, my mission is to provide you with as much information as I can, as quickly as I can. *This* book will provide an essential foundation for understanding the principles of loyalty so you can begin to build or refine your own loyalty strategies around it.

If you and your company have the determination, dedicated team, and commitment, there is no doubt you can build a first class loyalty program. Remember, this book is a tool, not a bible. Your loyalty strategy should complement your business, be it large or small. But be certain. Once you say go, hold on tight, because there's no turning back. **Initiating loyalty is an eternal strategy.**

Your loyalty strategy is without a doubt an unparalleled way for you to identify your customers and eventually change their purchasing behavior to become more profitable for your company.

Ironically, it is also the best way for you to learn about the strengths and weaknesses of your own business. So start off by being loyal to your customers, and give them a reason to be loyal in return.

Once you **GET** the fundamentals down, you will be on your way to mastering the art of loyalty. Start with the basics, and build your strategy around those values. As Coach Dunn told me, "Be loyal, and loyalty will be returned to you tenfold. It's a law of life."

—Roger L. Brooks

My Starbucks Rewards

ABOUT THE PROGRAM: Membership is free for My Starbucks Rewards; however, in order to participate you have to purchase a gift card for $5 or more and register your Starbucks Card online. There are three levels of membership, and members earn 1 Star for every purchase made with the card. The more stars you earn, the greater the rewards. Immediate perks for Welcome Level include a Free Drink on your birthday and up to two continuous hours of free daily WiFi.

WHAT I LIKE: You don't have to visit Starbucks every day to reap the benefits. It sets tiers so all customers can participate—even first-time visitors! As you graduate levels, the perks increase. Top-tier customers receive a personalized card for immediate recognition.

FOR MORE DETAILED INFORMATION VISIT:
starbucks.com/card

ALWAYS TREAT YOUR CUSTOMERS LIKE THEY'RE MADE OF GOLD!™

Recognize That Loyalty Is All Around You; It's EVERYWHERE Loyalty

IT'S REALLY NOT THAT COMPLICATED. Take a look around you—you are a consumer, and what you'll read in this book is not astrophysics. It's obvious you all know a little something about loyalty. I have lived and breathed it my entire career. It has become such a part of my being that an hour does not pass in a typical day when I'm not meeting, talking, writing, or thinking about LOYALTY.

So what is loyalty, and what is all the hype about? Adopting *loyalty* as a *strategy* is a philosophical transformation in your thinking. A *loyalty mind-set* is having a profound and deep belief in your product or service. *Loyalty* believes in your business, your employees, and your customers. *Loyalty* understands that there is give and take. *Loyalty* believes that investing in your customers will deliver return. Your loyalty strategy is a win-win proposition.

But what is the true definition of loyalty? Every company in every industry I have studied or worked with has its own. I'll examine a variety of factors that will assist you in determining your own definition or possibly modifying your current definition of loyalty. In the end, it's all about developing your own definition, applying that definition to your loyalty strategy, and motivating customer behavior as a means of reducing competition and increasing profits.

To better understand the basic definition of the word loyalty, let me acquaint you with its roots. According to Merriam-Webster.com, the word *loyalty* originates from the root word, *loyal*, which dates back to 1531. Below are the definitions of the words *loyal* and *loyalty*.

loy·al

1: unswerving in allegiance: as faithful to a cause, ideal, custom, institution, or product
2: showing loyalty

loy·al·ty

the quality or state or an instance of being loyal

By permission. From the *Merriam-Webster Online Dictionary* ©2010 by Merriam-Webster, Incorporated (Merriam-Webster.com).

What a remarkable definition for the word loyal: "unswerving in allegiance" and "faithful to a cause, ideal, custom, institution, or product." That is what you strive for every single day. You strive to win customer allegiance and faith in your brand.

So why not make things easier on yourself? Why not initiate a loyalty strategy and put the tools in place to assist you with your efforts?

When I think of the words *loyal* or *loyalty*, I also think of words such as *dedication, fidelity, reliability, dependability, constancy,* and *steadfastness*. I also think of the word *loyalty* when I think about how people are loyal to a particular cause, faith, sports team, family member, or spouse.

And as a consumer, it's amazing to think about the loyalty or *unswerving allegiance* you have and how *faithful* you are to specific brands or *products*. Loyalty is having the nerve and courage to stand behind a product, brand, or service in both good times and bad.

Everywhere you go, everything you do, and everything you decide to spend your hard-earned money on has some connection to customer loyalty.

People buy where they *feel good* buying. People spend where they *feel good* spending. The world is your personal selection of oysters, and you only open those which you feel most loyal to and where you feel you'll continue to find that shiny pearl you're always eager to uncover.

Understanding the intricacies of customer loyalty and the fundamental steps needed to build a successful customer loyalty strategy is an ongoing process. It cannot be learned overnight, nor can it be taught in its entirety in this book. Understanding loyalty and what creates customer loyalty is repetition, replication, recurrence, and reiteration.

Loyalty is constantly reminding your customers that they are valued. Loyalty is repeating your message as often as you can. There is no such thing as overemphasizing the recurrence and reiteration of your loyalty message to your customers. It is in that repetition where your message is reinforced.

You have to be creative in molding the information from this book into your own business. Your customer loyalty strategy will look much different if you are in the insurance industry versus retail. You know your business best, and you'll need to develop a strategy that fits best for your customers.

You will see later in the book that identifying your customers is the first step toward understanding who your customers are. Your industry, and to some extent the sophistication level of your systems, will dictate the ease of being able to identify your customers and in turn carry out your strategy. If you operate an online business, identifying your customers is much easier than if you operate a convenience store. Online businesses have an advantage because every customer provides an e-mail address that can be used as the loyalty identifier.

So, if you are in real estate or retail, fitness or finance, auto sales or antiques, there are basic steps you should follow to build a successful loyalty strategy. My commitment is to provide you with as much information as I can through this book series (and through my website), and save you time and money in the process.

Learn from the BEST

Throughout the book, you'll see various loyalty profiles featuring companies across multiple industries. You will recognize most of these companies, but some you will not. I carefully chose the companies included in order to demonstrate the vastness and diversity of loyalty programs currently in the marketplace. Some of the featured programs are pure rewards programs while others focus on unique loyalty strategies. Each of the programs has its own personal twist that makes it distinct. Learn from these programs, study them, and find ways to make your own loyalty strategy distinct.

Loyalty Is Reciprocal

The root of loyalty understands that loyalty is reciprocal. Loyalty is not one-sided. There is give and take with loyalty. You first have to demonstrate *your* loyalty to your customers before they will reciprocate by giving *their* loyalty in return. You have to prove that through each part of your business you are sincere about earning their trust. Practice consistency in everything you do, and you'll be on your way to earning the trust of your customers.

Encouraging your customers to choose you repeatedly over the competition is a marketing challenge that many organizations face. Differentiating yourself by enhancing your customers' buying experience can go a long way toward winning their long-term loyalty.

Typically, loyalty strategies are designed to identify who your customers are in order to track their activity and aim to change their purchasing behavior so they become more profitable to your bottom line.

Loyalty strategies can have many shapes, sizes, and meanings, but there are FIVE main principles of the loyalty cycle, which always remain constant. It is indeed a cycle as the process of each principle is never-ending.

1. Identify Customers
2. Track Spending
3. Motivate Behavior
4. Reward Performance
5. Measure Results

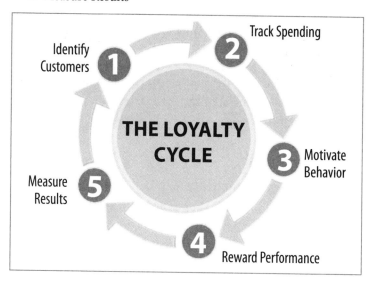

Sophisticated customers today watch their spending closely and expect more in return. Given a choice, they would rather spend their hard-earned dollars with a company that values their business while having an opportunity to earn rewards and benefits over time.

So what's your company doing to improve the complete buying experience? What's your strategy for acquiring new customers and retaining existing ones? How can you increase the profitability of your customers' transactions? The short answer to these questions is this: Initiate a loyalty strategy.

If you follow the basic principles of the loyalty cycle, the success of your loyalty program will speak for itself. Your loyal customers will frequent you more often and increase spending, which will lead to greater profitability. And you're never too large or too small to launch a loyalty program. Whether you have three stores or 300, a bakery or a bank, you can design a loyalty program that complements your current business strategy.

Below is a brief description of each principle within the loyalty cycle. An expanded version of each principle is found in Essential Steps 6 through 10.

1. Identify Customers

All loyalty programs must have a means of identifying customers. Initiate a process to identify your customers, and assign a unique identifier to each (i.e., loyalty card, payment instrument, e-mail address, etc.). The loyalty program identifier is the linchpin to your program.

2. Track Spending

Once an identifier is in place, you now have the means to track spending. Numerous loyalty applications can do this. Talk to your point-of-sale provider, credit card processor, or IT department to research and implement reliable and stable loyalty tracking software.

3. Motivate Behavior

Identifying your customers and tracking their spending provide an ideal platform for motivating customer behavior. After compiling a minimum of two to three months of historical data, you can start to analyze the data, market directly to your loyal customers, and aim to change their purchasing behavior.

4. Reward Performance

People like to be rewarded for their performance. If the reward has a high perceived value, then your customer will more likely take action.

5. Measure Results

All of the previous steps are irrelevant if you can't measure results. Loyalty programs evolve based on the success of individual promotions and campaigns within your strategy. Once you can measure the results of each promotion, you can measure the success of your loyalty strategy.

Over time, a well-thought-out loyalty strategy can pay itself back and provide a true return on investment (ROI). Once you put the tools in place to initiate the five principles of the loyalty cycle, your loyalty program will provide the basic foundation for you to nurture customers, build the program, and reap the benefits.

The **1st ESSENTIAL STEP** to Build a Successful Customer Loyalty Strategy is to RECOGNIZE THAT LOYALTY IS ALL AROUND YOU; IT'S *EVERYWHERE LOYALTY!*

Everywhere Loyalty describes the consumer-driven world you live in. If you look close enough, loyalty is visible everywhere you go and part of everything you do.

Everywhere Loyalty refers to the coffee shop you frequent, the bank you deposit with, the restaurants you dine in, the real estate agent you buy from, the pharmacy you choose—and all of the other touch points and places you patronize in between because they are the best fit for you. You remain loyal because there's *something* about each one of them that keeps you coming back. The reason you remain loyal may be price or it may be the product or even the person you interact with, but each of these places provides some sort of motivation for you to keep coming back, some sort of motivation for you to remain loyal.

Think about it. For the most part, you have endless choices when it comes to making purchases. It's not always easy choosing which restaurant, office supply house, home improvement store, or gas station to patronize. There are so many options today that choosing where you spend your hard-earned dollars can sometimes be overwhelming. But you do ultimately choose—be it for location, convenience, price, or any other motivator. You choose for a reason that can likely be traced back to the personal reasons you remain loyal. Oftentimes, you may even choose because you participate in a loyalty program and feel attached in that way.

Businesses have been trying for decades to master the art of earning and then maintaining a customer's loyalty. Some businesses have truly mastered the art, but most have not. **How many companies do you do business with that can improve their sales process, customer service, or delivery of their product or service?** Most companies have room for improvement. Improving business practices leads to greater customer loyalty, which is a task that many companies work very hard to achieve. If the magic formula is found, constant maintenance and dedication are required to retain such high service levels to keep customers loyal.

You all participate in loyalty programs in one form or another. More than likely you currently participate in one or more of the following programs: airline, hotel, grocery, pharmacy, sporting goods, credit card, bookstore, office supply, restaurant, gas station, department store, coffee shop, shoe store, etc. If you want to get a more detailed listing of the specific programs you are enrolled in, simply look in your wallet or hold up your key chain. That should provide a friendly reminder.

Why is loyalty, and loyalty strategy in particular, such a big part of engaging customer behavior? Because at the end of the day, each consumer and each one of you want to feel appreciated and enjoy receiving a reward for your constant patronage. You enjoy being loyal, but you also enjoy receiving return benefits for your loyalty.

DIFFICULT QUESTION: *Why are there so many different loyalty programs?*

SIMPLE ANSWER: *Because if administered properly, loyalty programs work. Here's why:*

Loyalty programs provide a competitive advantage.

Loyalty programs are a "hook" to keep customers coming back.

Loyalty programs help identify your most profitable customers.

Loyalty programs can positively alter purchasing behavior.

Loyalty programs help lead to more profitable customers.

I'd like you to take a quick test. To demonstrate loyalty in its purist form, I'm going to list ten products or brands I am most loyal to. On a scrap piece of paper or on the blank lines next to mine, I'd like you to do the same. List **TEN** products or brands you're most loyal to.

1. Miami Dolphins _____
2. iPhone _____
3. Nike _____
4. Starbucks _____
5. New York Yankees _____
6. Zappos.com _____
7. Titleist _____
8. Versace ties _____
9. Nordstrom _____
10. *Entrepreneur* magazine _____

Show your list to three people you have a close relationship with. As they are reading through the list, ask them who the list represents. I guarantee you'll receive the same answer from all three people. "I think of *you*," they'll say.

It's remarkable how such a simple exercise can define the essence of the products and brands you are most loyal to. It defines the person you are as a consumer and most likely represents the ten products or brands you obviously think of first and most often.

The Power of Loyalty

Here are the reasons I am loyal to the products and brands I chose.

- *I like the Miami Dolphins because my father was and still is a Miami Dolphins fan. I grew up a Dolphins fan, and I don't know anything different. I also like that they are the only undefeated team in the history of the NFL (which I like to point out in heated football discussions).*

- *I like the iPhone because I think it is the greatest invention of my lifetime, and it is my primary source of communication, relaxation, and entertainment. My iPhone is by my side every minute of every day.*

- *I like Nike because I spent six years in Portland, Oregon, where the company was founded, and I feel a personal connection to Phil Knight and the brand. I also like the high quality of its clothes and shoes.*

- *I like Starbucks Coffee because I consider it my first experience and introduction to loyalty. I also like its nonfat mocha and its blueberry crumb cake.*

- *I like the New York Yankees because they attract the biggest stars in the game and play on the biggest stage in the history of sports.*

- *I like Zappos.com because it has the most humble approach to customer loyalty of any company that I know. I also like that its service is second to none. I really like that there is always free shipping.*

- *I like Titleist golf balls because they are the best golf balls made. I also make more putts when I use the Titleist ball.*

Roger L. Brooks

- *I like Versace ties because my mother-in-law bought me one about ten years ago and I felt more confident when I wore that tie. I now own over 20 Versace ties.*

- *I like Nordstrom because I feel good shopping there, especially the Nordstrom at the King of Prussia Mall in King of Prussia, Pennsylvania. I also like when the clerk walks around the counter to hand me the bag after I make a purchase.*

- *I like Entrepreneur magazine because I enjoy the articles and insights on progressive companies and individuals with cutting-edge ventures. I also like that Entrepreneur Press is the publisher of this book.*

Once you finish this exercise, I believe you will agree it would be quite easy to be a spokesperson for any of the brands or products you list. Once you become loyal to a product or brand, it's hard to pull away from that brand. It becomes a part of your fiber and makes up the person you are.

That is why companies spend ungodly amounts of money trying to earn greater market share and to retain customer loyalty. It's also precisely the reason companies know where and when to draw the line.

If a customer survey found that a customer leased a new Cadillac every 4 years for the past 12 years, chances are he will not be purchasing a Lincoln as his next car. However, if the incentive has enough value to make someone switch, a customer's loyalty to a particular brand can be challenged. That is exactly the reason you can never take a customer's loyalty for granted. It's a tough balance, and maintaining a loyal customer base requires that your company excel in many areas, hence underscoring the need for perfecting the complete loyalty experience.

Personal Relationships Yield Loyalty

Take a quick moment to recall where you have your dry cleaning serviced. There's a reason you go to a particular cleaner. Whatever the reason, it can be traced back to the loyalty you have toward that business. Unless you live in a rural area, there are a number of dry cleaning businesses to choose from.

I choose to go to Martin Brothers Cleaners. Martin Brothers is not the cheapest, and it is not the closest to my home. I go because I'm satisfied with the cleaning service and because I like the owner, George. I go because George made a connection with me. The first time I went into his store he was polite, he was efficient, and he was friendly. The second time I went in, George called me by name. He also brought out a sealed envelope with my name written on it. In the envelope was $16 in cash he said he found in my pants pocket. In only two visits, George captured me as a customer for life.

Today, more than ten years later, George is as friendly and courteous as he was on my first visit. George's positive attitude led him to earn my loyalty to him and to his business.

In essence, George's personality has everything to do with why I am loyal to his dry cleaning business. Although it may be the simplest form of customer loyalty, connecting with customers on a one-to-one basis may be the most important. If George had a personality that didn't mesh well with his customers or allow him to connect with them in some personal way, there would be a certain percentage of his customer base he would not retain.

Having a positive attitude goes a long way. If the people you have on the front line—the cashiers, the CSRs, the waitstaff, the Wal-Mart greeters, the fuel attendant, the bank teller, or the gallery curator—are not your "A TEAM," then you're putting your business at risk right from the start. You may not lose business at the particular moment when the cashier wouldn't crack a smile; however, you're losing future business from a potential loyal customer who wants to be treated with respect for choosing your business over your competitor.

If you want to build your loyal base of customers, start by treating customers the way you would want to be treated yourself. Your gut-check is always the best indicator of whether your customers are being treated as well as they should be. Look around, observe how your staff interacts with your customers—you'll know if there's room for improvement.

George found that treating people well is the magic formula to his success as a small-business owner. His formula, or his loyalty strategy, consists of being courteous, friendly, efficient, honest, and dry cleaning clothes to the best of his ability. George comes in early, he leaves late, and he works six days a week. He also operates in two locations. Hard work and dedication pay dividends, which leads to earning a customer's loyalty.

The same basic principles apply whether you are an entrepreneur with a small chain of gas and convenience stores or a large department store with hundreds of locations. Your employees (associates, clerks, CSRs, or whatever you refer to them as) are your first touch point to the consumer. Ensure they do the little things for your customers that will leave a lasting impression and set the groundwork for earning their loyalty.

Connecting One-to-One

Like most couples, my wife and I enjoy dining out alone as well as dining out with our family and friends. We are attracted to restaurants that have a combination of great food, fine atmosphere, and outstanding service. Of all the restaurants we frequent, good service is the one area I find least consistent. There are many factors that lead to poor service, but it comes down to properly training your staff so they treat people as well as they would like to be treated themselves. Business owners work hard, especially small-business owners, and in order to keep a loyal customer base, exceptional service is key, and having the proper staff can make all the difference in the world to your bottom line.

When we do find a server we connect with we'll often request that person by name. I'll use Cortese Restaurant, located in Binghamton, New York, as an example. The food at Cortese is always consistent, the atmosphere is always pleasant. When we dine at Cortese, we always

If the people you have on the front line are not your "A TEAM," then you're putting your business at risk right from the start.

request our favorite waiter, Andy. To me, Andy is the face of Cortese. Andy is always consistent. He is always friendly, funny, and conscious of our needs as customers. Andy is not too pushy, and he's very attentive. He takes our order, he asks how the kids are, he brings our drinks quickly, and he is attuned to each person as they place their order. Because Andy takes the time to listen to his customers' needs, he very rarely makes mistakes. He'll recommend a specific dish if it is out of this world, and he'll advise if a certain dish doesn't look the greatest on a particular day.

As much as I enjoy Cortese, its fabulous pizza, pork chops, and other dishes, it wouldn't be the same without Andy. We are loyal to Cortese, but we are equally loyal to Andy. Because of Andy, we go back time and again.

Your wait staff or equivalent is the face of your business, and strict attention must be paid to those placed in roles that interact directly with customers. There are many small but significant efforts that can lead to retaining a customer and keeping that customer loyal—and that effort starts with your people.

If you ever want a truly memorable pizza, order a Cortese Pizza online. It'll ship it to you overnight frozen on dry ice. Pop it in the oven for 30 minutes, and it's ready to eat. Visit corteserestaurant.com.

Whether it's George the dry cleaner or Andy the waiter, it's important to have a friendly and courteous staff prepared to welcome your customers. The foundation of loyalty includes keeping sight of the important blocking and tackling needed to run the business. Consumers long for consistency and reliability. Consumers want to know they can count on your business to satisfy their needs. Consumers will remain loyal knowing they will get what they expect in return.

STEP 1

GOLDEN TIPS

1. Define what loyalty means for your business.

2. Recognize that loyalty is everywhere around you.

3. Be attentive to the many choices customers have today, and give them a reason to buy from you.

4. List the items you can improve on in your business to build customer loyalty.

5. Loyalty is reciprocal. Start out by being loyal to your customers, and you'll see how they will become loyal in return.

6. Your business is only as good as your people. Put your A TEAM in front of your customers every day.

7. Personal relationships yield loyalty.

T.G.I. Friday's®
Give Me More Stripes®

ABOUT THE PROGRAM: There are immediate benefits and there is no fee to join. Upon sign-up (online, interactive jukebox or by texting JOIN to MYTGIF), guests receive a Jump the Line Pass and a certificate for a free appetizer or dessert, and members will begin earning one "stripe" for every dollar spent on all purchases with food. For every $100 spent, members will receive an $8 coupon for free food. There is no limit to that.

WHAT I LIKE: They do know how to keep things fun, but it's more than that. Friday's® is the party headquarters. From its charismatic and refreshing team members to its exciting rewards program, dining at Friday's has its perks. There are no limits on the amount you can earn, and it'll continue to reward and recognize you with extras in a variety of ways throughout the year. Friday's routinely sends members-only coupons and advance notice of new menu items as well as a variety of other valuable offers and special events.

FOR MORE DETAILED INFORMATION VISIT: www.givememorestripes.com

Roger L. Brooks

Know Your Customers; Treat Them Like They're Made of GOLD

YOU'VE ALL EXPERIENCED THE SURPRISE and delight of being treated like a *valued* customer. There is no better feeling than being pampered when buying a new pair of shoes or being attended to when trying to find a cold medicine at the pharmacy. On the flip side, there is no worse feeling than being pushed too hard, ignored, or even unnoticed when you are ready to buy. Staying attentive to your customers' needs is a tough and delicate balance, and it is a key component to achieving customer approval and earning a customer's loyalty. Treating your customers like they're made of GOLD is the next layer in the foundation of building your loyalty strategy.

In order to win your customers' confidence and eventually win their loyalty, there's a prerequisite needed: Tactfully demonstrate that each customer is valued and treat her as such.

Over the years, I've attended many customer loyalty sessions, conferences, and seminars. The general consensus is that you should focus a majority of your resources on your most loyal and profitable customers. While it's vitally important to focus resources on your most loyal customers, it's equally important to place value on all customers. There's also a direct effect on properly training your employees so they can help carry out your goals to promote customer loyalty and your customer loyalty initiatives.

As you've likely observed, this entire book is dedicated to a theme of GOLD. The reason, as outlined in the title of this chapter, is that loyalty, customer loyalty, and loyalty programs have a direct effect on how customers are treated.

If you treat all your customers like they are truly valued or like they are made of GOLD, they will react accordingly. The "GOLD" theme in this book is a constant reminder to treasure the business each customer contributes to your bottom line. If you do, customers will return that special treatment in repeat business as a loyal customer. The ultimate goal in business is to earn your customers' trust and their lifelong loyalty. Fulfilling that goal will result in increased profits, which underscores the fact that treating customers like GOLD will garner the same.

The reason you're in business is to grow your customer base and continually increase profits. Every business strives to capture more market share. Making modifications in how you treat your new and existing customers can be the most cost-effective way to increase your profits. So before you initiate or enhance your customer loyalty strategy, it's very important that the entire organization adopt a policy to treat each and every customer as they would want to be treated themselves.

Treating customers like they're made of GOLD will yield:

Allegiance

Devotion

Commitment

Support

Promise

Dedication

LOYALTY!

Treating customers like they're made of gold is the essence of customer loyalty. It reinforces why loyalty is reciprocal. If your product or service continues to exceed customer expectations and your company has a fundamental practice of valuing each customer, you will succeed in your mission of achieving exceptional customer loyalty.

KNOW YOUR CUSTOMERS. It's surprising that a high percentage of companies do not know or care to know who their customers actually are. Many companies simply see customers as dollar signs and avoid any personal connection beyond the transaction itself. One of the most basic practices of any business *should be* to know your customers because without them you'll have no business. It's not that you need to know the name of every person who enters your place of business, calls your office, or visits your website each day, but you should have tools in place to be able to gain some intelligence about your customers in order to effectively service or upsell them. Learning more about your customers helps build better relationships that lead to increased business.

How can you learn more about your customers?

Listen to their needs.

The **2nd ESSENTIAL STEP** to Build a Successful Customer Loyalty Strategy is to KNOW YOUR CUSTOMERS; TREAT THEM LIKE THEY'RE MADE OF GOLD.

Like all relationships, in order to get to know and better understand your customers and their needs, it is important to start by gathering relevant information about them and their spending habits. Having better insight into their buying preferences allows you to market to them in a more relevant way.

You have all heard the old adage that people will tell only one person about a positive experience versus telling ten people about a negative one. Assuming that is true, it is all the more reason to treat all customers equally. If you only focus on those customers you *feel* are your most profitable customers, you may be alienating a large customer segment and potentially forfeiting potential business by simply not treating people better. This is especially true and becomes more obvious when you have a mechanism in place to track customer spending and behavior. Frequently, it is the customers you may least expect that are actually your most profitable customers in the end.

Mystery shoppers or mystery callers should play a key role in your loyalty strategy. Mystery shoppers are hired to pose as regular customers while they take certain actions such as buying a product, asking for assistance, or even voicing a complaint. Then, the mystery shopper or caller will evaluate her experience and measure the quality of service received. The feedback you receive will be crucial in order to continue to improve your tactics.

Treat ALL customers equally.

Value each customer, as each contributes to your bottom line.

Show appreciation for all purchases, large and small.

Have a formal process in place to personally thank customers for their business.

Consider how your business can begin to reward loyal customers for their continued patronage.

Purchasing habits are sometimes unpredictable. It is better to service each customer to the best of your ability so each can be valued for the business they bring. Anything less is unacceptable.

Where Did We Go Wrong?

Looking back on our nation's history, I'm not sure exactly when we lost common decency and respect for our fellow man. There were obviously many cultural and political changes and advancements that took place over the decades that had both positive and negative effects on where we are today. Without getting too philosophical, it seems the business community as a whole has lost many basic fundamentals in treating customers with common decency and respect—even in this highly competitive consumer-driven world we live in.

Our country has lost a great deal of ground in the common decency category, and it is going to be a challenge to make it up. You can, however, do your part to improve the level of respect your employees show for your customers in your respective business. Common decency and respect return loyalty. It seems so basic, doesn't it?

Consumers remember their experiences. They tend to complain about negative experiences more than they brag about positive experiences. Negative experiences can dominate their thoughts, and negative thoughts have a direct effect on purchasing behavior.

So how do businesses keep their employees positive and focused on each individual customer so that each experience is a positive and pleasant one? It's not easy.

Training Is Key

To start, management must commit to a training program that affords employees the necessary tools and resources to learn the corporate culture and implement it in everyday customer interaction. Quite often companies do not take the time for adequate training, and employees are left in the dark, making their own decisions on how to interact with customers.

A committed training program should ensure that employees are well versed in understanding the company's core philosophies. Employees should also have a thorough understanding of the company's products or service as well as the company goals and mission statement.

Companies that provide employees with solid training and communicate company policies, procedures, and goals on a frequent basis tend to come out on top in customer satisfaction. Instituting these best practices is an important part of building a solid loyalty strategy.

Promote ongoing communication to employees. Employees will quickly understand they can rely on their company when organized communication channels are in place. Many companies do this through weekly e-mail updates, company newsletters, or even scheduled conference calls where employees can listen in and participate by asking questions. Employees will remain more focused on company goals when they are kept informed.

Once training and communication are in place, employees will begin to believe and trust in the company culture. They will buy into the company philosophy, which is crucial to your overall plan.

I don't have to tell you what follows. Once you have buy-in from your employees, you now have the total package, and that translates to employee PERFORMANCE. Employee performance will breed better results and consequently equate to more loyal customers.

Training + Communication = Buy-in

Buy-in = Performance

Performance = Loyal Customers

Like Albert Einstein's formula of mass-energy equivalence ($E = MC^2$), I believe a similar conclusion occurs when you examine the effect of loyalty.

$$L = MP^2$$

LOYALTY = the MAGNITUDE of PERFORMANCE^2

Here's the secret formula to measure loyalty. In order to measure loyalty, multiply the magnitude by the square of performance. I'll repeat, multiply the magnitude by the square of performance.

OK, you can stop scratching your head now. I am being facetious; there is no true mathematical formula to measure loyalty. However, if you were able to measure loyalty with such a formula, I believe it would be similar to what the formula suggests.

Think of it this way. Performance has an exponential effect on the success of your business. Investing twice the amount of ample and sufficient training in your employees should return at least four times the investment. If employees are properly trained and demonstrate exceptional performance, that performance will return a multiple of that training back to the company in the form of loyal customers. As you now know, loyal customers equate to increased profits.

I firmly believe that if your company adopts these values and puts significant resources into your people, you can be as successful as you want to be and reap the rewards of the customer's loyalty in return.

Apple Anyone?

I wanted to put one of today's hottest brands to the GOLD-TEST. My objective was to see how the retail customer experience related to a product that was on top of its game. Over the course of a three-month period, I visited seven separate Apple Stores in five cities in search of an Apple iTouch.

I made a commitment to myself that I wouldn't purchase the product until I was completely satisfied with the overall customer experience. I wanted to be certain the experience would be as good as, or better than, the product itself. I visited stores in Tampa, Orlando, Philadelphia, Manhattan, and Syracuse.

No pressure, high confidence **approach.** On each occasion, every Apple store I walked into was jam-packed with customers. While in Tampa on business, I went into the Apple Store at International Plaza. The first thing I noticed was that the store had plenty of workers—all wearing color coordinated T-shirts. I took a walk from the front of the store to the back and returned to the front. In less than three minutes, four separate sales associates approached me. What I liked most was that the associates had a *no pressure, high confidence* approach. No pressure toward me as the buyer, and high confidence by them as the seller. While engaged in conversation with one of the sales associates, I felt no pressure to buy until I was 100 percent satisfied with my buying decision.

Apple passed the GOLD-TEST with flying colors. Like Starbucks, the Apple associates all treated me as if I were the most important customer to them at that moment. They were not concerned with my age and could care less about my dress code. They ensured that my purchase was a memorable one and closed the experience by asking if I would like a paper receipt or an e-mail receipt. I chose to receive the e-mail receipt. Before I could exit the store, the receipt was sitting in the inbox on my cell phone.

If I were to guess the marching orders from the Apple corporate office to all Apple sales associates, I'm sure it would look something like this:

1. Know our products inside and out before you step on our dance floor.
2. Treat every customer equally as you do not know when he'll buy or how much he has to spend.
3. While in uniform: Smile, and be attentive, courteous, and helpful.
4. Apple products are superior and somewhat intimidating. Let the customer ask questions and respond accordingly.
5. Don't stand around. Move swiftly and confidently-action sells.

I learned something from Apple through this experimental self-test. Apple is as passionate about how it treats its customers as it is about its products. It understands the importance of both, and how both lead to a loyal following.

Businesses that succeed treat each and every customer as if she is the most important customer in the world. They treat their customers like they're **MADE OF GOLD**!

Value Your Customers

In the mid- to late-1990s, I worked on a loyalty program for the Bell Atlantic Telephone Company. At that time, competition was fierce between the "baby bells" and the long-distance giants as deregulation was rampant in the industry.

The baby bell companies, including Bell Atlantic, were trying to defend their territory while companies such as AT&T and MCI were aggressively going after local market share.

The long-distance giants were offering customers $100 checks to simply switch their local service to them. Bell Atlantic and others could not compete with the high-priced incentive to switch, so instead they decided to conduct focus groups with their customers to see what incentives would be needed to maintain customer loyalty.

Overwhelmingly, customers told Bell Atlantic they wanted valuable offers from merchants where they shopped and dined. The customers in the focus group asked for items such as gas cards, movie tickets, and pizza deals. Customers also said they wanted significant savings at local merchants on everyday purchases.

The outcome of the focus groups concluded that the best way to compete with the long-distance giants was to provide a product with immense value and relevance to each customer. Bell Atlantic challenged our company at that time (Dine-A-Mate, Inc.) to aggregate local and regional merchant offerings in the following categories: dining, recreation, services, and travel. We completed the task and combined valuable merchant discount offers into a savings guide, called *Local Values*. The guide contained hundreds of dollars in savings. Utilizing a data process called *geocoding*, our company provided Bell Atlantic with maps plotted with various layers of symbols consisting of customers and merchants by category. This exercise proved the relevance of the offers as Bell Atlantic overlaid them against its customer database.

The goal of providing merchant offers pertinent to the average customer was achieved, and Bell Atlantic was able to use the Local Values books as both a retention and customer loyalty tool.

One of the challenges with the program was deciding which customers would and would not receive the books. Bell Atlantic decided to focus its efforts on its top-tier customers based on monthly spending. Those customers who had an average monthly spending level within the decided threshold were included in the program. Customers with less financial value were not included. The only exception was that any Bell Atlantic customer inquiring about the book was sent a copy—no questions asked.

The books were packaged in a slick blue and green cardboard carton (the company's corporate colors). Inside the customer found a welcome letter explaining the details of the program, and an optional customer survey was accompanied with a self-addressed stamped envelope. The welcome letter also let customers know how valuable they were to Bell Atlantic and how much the company appreciated their business. The program was extremely well received.

Not only were the offers in the books valuable, they were relevant to where customers lived, worked, shopped, and dined. Bell Atlantic was known as the neighborhood telephone company and therefore wanted to make sure that any offers it provided to its customers were significant and within their footprint.

Customers raved about Local Values. The books drove millions of dollars of commerce into the local marketplace as customers frequented the local steak house, dry cleaner, auto service station, bowling alley, symphony, and ballpark.

The loyalty program was deemed a tremendous success and lasted for nearly three years until GTE and Bell Atlantic merged in 2000 to form Verizon Communications, Inc. Bell Atlantic listened to its customers and responded to them by providing a more compelling offer than the competition, and at a fraction of the price.

Several months into the program, the Bell Atlantic team sent us a large envelope containing thousands of survey responses received from customers. Customers overwhelmingly expressed their appreciation to Bell Atlantic for sending such a significant and worthwhile gift. Customers raved about receiving something for nothing. Customers thanked Bell Atlantic for being thanked—pretty ironic.

This program is a perfect example that when you listen, value, and treat your customers like GOLD, that effort will go a long way toward earning long-term loyalty.

There are many cost-effective ways to gather information about your customers and their needs. Here are SIX thoughts on how to capture more information about your customers:

1. Conduct customer surveys.
2. Utilize receipt/e-mail messaging.
3. Conduct focus groups.
4. Run a sweepstakes.
5. Analyze transaction history.
6. Organize post-sale courtesy calls.

Bell Atlantic listened to its customers and responded to them by providing a more compelling offer than its competition.

There is no better way to find out about your customers than talking directly to them and finding out what their *wants* and *needs* truly are.

Customer surveys may sound trivial as a means of gathering information about your customers, but they are vitally important *if* you ask the right questions. Customer surveys are a relatively simple and inexpensive way to gather important information. They are very useful once you have a loyalty program in place. The most crucial part of making the customer survey effective is taking the time to make sure you're asking the right series of questions.

Recently I worked with a convenience store operator who was launching a loyalty program. In order for customers to join the program, they were required to fill out an enrollment form and survey. First, the operator gathered mandatory information such as customer name, address, zip code, e-mail address, and cellular telephone number. (See the importance of capturing these mandatory fields in Essential Step 6.) Then the operator asked a series of questions on the reverse side of the enrollment form in order to try to gather intelligence about the customer and serve them better.

Customer surveys can be vitally important
IF
you ask the right questions!

I'd like to share the questions with you. Consider how they can be adapted in a survey for your business:

1. What convenience stores do you visit on a regular basis?
2. What types of items are you most likely to purchase?
3. What method of payment do you normally use?
4. How do you rate our "Full Service" gas service?
5. What types of rewards are important to you?
6. Are you currently a member of any other rewards programs? If so, what programs?
7. Would you like us to offer online shopping?
8. Would you like us to offer in-store pickup service?
9. What food items would you like us to carry?
10. What areas can we improve upon?

As customers enroll in this loyalty program and provide answers to the survey questions, the responses will be recorded into the customer's data profile. At a later date, the survey information will become an essential piece of information for the overall loyalty strategy.

Sample E-Mail

Dear Mr. Trager:

Thank you for being a valued customer. I wanted you to be one of our first loyal customers to know that we are now offering in-store pickup service on select in-store purchases on such items as eggs, milk, and bread. You told us that you had an interest in pickup service and we responded.

If you place your first order within the next 14 days, we will provide you with 25 cents off per gallon (up to 20 gallons) on your next fill-up! Plus you will receive 100 BONUS POINTS!

Simply click on the link below to place your pickup order, choose your pickup location, and pay with any major credit card. We'll have your order ready for you for the time you choose. As an added bonus, use the enclosed coupon for a free loaf of bread on your order of $20 or more compliments of Stroehmann!

Thank you for your continued business, and thank you for being a valued customer!

Sincerely,

Mr. Convenience Store Owner

The survey promoted opportunity for new revenue by offering a service which didn't exist previous to the survey. It also provided for involvement from a vendor (Stroehmann's) which assisted in offsetting a portion of the promotion. Advertising can be sold as part of the survey and subsequent e-mail communications.

Being superior in attentiveness, responsiveness, and overall customer service results in a more loyal customer base. Learning more about your customers, by listening and responding to them, will aid you in your quest to build a rich database of loyal customers.

Take a fresh approach, and lead by example. **Communicate your message to every employee and put the company's focus back on the customer.** The results may just surprise you.

Know your customers, treat them well, and your business will earn the right to an exponential return.

Verizon Perks

ABOUT THE PROGRAM: Enjoy the benefits of Verizon Perks, where you can save more before you shop. Access its Gift Card Gallery where you can buy top brand cards online for your favorite stores and restaurants—for up to 10 percent off. The gift cards are delivered straight to your door!

WHAT I LIKE: Verizon provides its customers with ongoing savings at national brand merchants such as Regal Cinemas, Barnes & Noble, Bath & Body Works, Golfsmith, Lands' End, Kmart, and Macy's, as well as many restaurants including P.F. Chang's, Romano's Macaroni Grill, Roy's, and Outback Steakhouse. Verizon promises to add more perks for its home phone, internet, and TV customers including the hottest new content, free product sample offers, and the opportunity to be the first to know about new products and services.

FOR MORE DETAILED INFORMATION VISIT:
verizon.com/value

STEP 2

GOLDEN TIPS

1. Stay attentive to your customers.

2. Treat each and every customer as if they're made of GOLD.

3. Common decency and respect return loyalty.

4. Adopt a no pressure, high confidence sales approach.

5. Challenge your company to pass the GOLD-TEST.

6. LOYALTY = the MASS of PERFORMANCE^2.

7. Be as passionate about your customer service as you are about your product or service.

8. Each buying experience should be a memorable one for your customers.

9. Talk to your customers, survey them, and listen to their wants and needs—then respond accordingly.

Loyalty Starts from the Top

Loyalty Starts from the TOP

So YOU THINK YOU CAN launch a loyalty program strategy without the overall acceptance, approval, and buy-in from the CEO? **WRONG!**

A loyalty strategy is not a *trendy* new approach to your marketing plan. If you are serious about making loyalty work as intended, your loyalty strategy **BECOMES** your marketing strategy. Unless you're the CEO or equivalent, don't waste your time performing research or due diligence until you are certain you have total company buy-in and that instituting a loyalty program is *the* direction the COMPANY wants to take.

The **3rd ESSENTIAL STEP** to Build a Successful Customer Loyalty Strategy is understanding **LOYALTY STARTS FROM THE TOP**.

One of the most important factors when initiating your strategy is to tap into the overall brainpower your company has to offer, starting with the CEO. The CEO did not get where he is by accident. Tap into as much intelligence at the highest level as early in the process as you can. This will help to eliminate unnecessary research and effort on your part, AND it will put you in good standing with the overall loyalty program initiative out of the gate.

YOU are the offensive coordinator. You were just hired to be the offensive coordinator for the New York Giants, and you have seven months to prepare for the season. Every day, you work with the offensive coaching staff to develop and refine the plays so that the team is ready to perform without hesitation with your new offense come opening day. All the players buy into your new offense, and they run the plays to perfection in training camp. All cylinders are working, but you left out the most important piece. You didn't discuss the details of the new offense with the head coach. You never received his stamp of approval on your offensive direction. You never bothered to consider if your vision was also his vision.

Unfortunately, the head coach sees running the offense a bit differently than you do as it relates to the overall strategy for the team. Two weeks into training camp he drops a playbook on your desk and asks you to go back to the offense the team ran the previous three years. Several weeks of preparation and effort suddenly come to a halt, and now you're scrambling, playing defense to get your team ready to play offense. It's a big mess, a big waste of time, and the fact that you overlooked consulting with the head coach from the beginning could potentially cost you your job.

The same holds true in the business world. When you want to make a fundamental change in the way your company operates, seek approval at the top first. Initiating a loyalty program requires changes in employee mind-set, marketing strategy, and core operations. Before you spend time laying the groundwork for the loyalty program, ensure that the CEO and the entire company will embrace the strategy. Be sure the direction is not only your direction but the direction of the CEO or highest ranking officer in the company.

Consulting the CEO from the outset will:

Start the program off on the right foot.

Save you time and hassle.

Enable proper use of resources.

Promote company wide acceptance.

When you meet with the CEO, be prepared to state your case for initiating a loyalty program strategy. Typically, the first question a CEO will ask is, "Why do we need to have a loyalty program?"

Here's Why:
Because Loyalty Programs

Build awareness.

Build brand equity.

Build customer approval.

Build customer appreciation.

Build a competitive advantage.

Build a greater knowledge of your products/services.

Loyalty programs provide tools to gain greater intelligence about your customers and provide a means to target specific segments of your customer base while attempting to change purchasing behavior.

Your CEO may then say, "Our customers are very satisfied with the service we provide. Isn't that enough?"

No, and here's why. Satisfaction on its own does not equate to earning customer loyalty. Having a new loyalty strategy in place will increase overall customer satisfaction as you begin to implement specific promotions and campaigns that talk directly to your customers as individuals. You will need to clearly outline for your CEO specific examples of how your loyalty strategy will positively impact your customers and your business.

Before meeting with your CEO regarding your loyalty strategy ask yourself these FOUR questions:

1. Is there an immediate need or sense of urgency to create a loyalty program strategy in order to acquire new or retain your existing customers (or both)?

2. Is your company searching for opportunities to better service your customers while aiming to increase their profitability?

3. Does it make good business sense for your company to launch a loyalty program based on the line of business you're in?

4. Is the CEO and management team ready and prepared for a change in the way your business markets to your customers?

If you answered yes to one or more of the questions, you are ready to move on to the next phase.

Here are SIX important steps you can take to ensure loyalty is embraced from the top down:

1. Once you outline your general loyalty program strategy, schedule an initial meeting with your management team and CEO to discuss the concept of a loyalty program.

2. Record and discuss all of the pros and cons on launching a loyalty program.

3. Meet with your technology team early on to determine any potential financial impact the program will have on your technical infrastructure. Also determine what the approximate time will be to have the technology ready to launch your loyalty program.

4. Meet with your marketing team to discuss the overall direction of the loyalty program. Keep in mind that the loyalty program *should* become your marketing strategy.

5. Meet with your accounting team to discuss important financial matters related to the loyalty program. Be sure to discuss and include the rewards component and liability of the program.

6. Meet with your customer service manager and outline what customer service changes need to be made to accommodate all facets of customer service as it relates to the loyalty program strategy.

A complete blueprint of your loyalty strategy is required, start to finish, so that the entire process is structured and organized as you prepare to launch your initiative.

Once you're fully prepared and have a blueprint of the program, meet again with the CEO to state your case for the loyalty initiative. Solicit support from each department head. Address all potential risks and challenges, and demonstrate how the loyalty strategy will positively impact your company as a whole.

As soon as your company has worked through all the critical issues and a decision is made to move forward, it's time to set the groundwork for company wide acceptance of the loyalty strategy.

Here are THREE ideas to get you started:

1. Draft a letter for the CEO to approve and sign. Then, distribute the letter to each employee. Include the letter inside each employee's paycheck, if possible. The letter should set the stage for the loyalty program strategy and provide a high-level overview and a message that more information will be forthcoming.

2. Within one week, provide each employee with a more detailed overview of the program strategy. The overview can be sent via e-mail if available. If not, a one-page flier, front and back, will work. The overview should include:

   * The reasons the company has decided to launch a loyalty program.

   * The official name and logo of the loyalty program.

   * An overview of the structure of the program including what will be used as the program currency (points, cash back, instant rewards) and how enrollment will take place.

- The anticipated launch date of the loyalty program.

- A list of the loyalty program benefits for customers.

- A list of the loyalty program benefits for employees.

- A list of the loyalty program rewards or redemption items.

3. Provide an internal loyalty program e-mail address where employees can submit their ideas to enhance or ask questions about the program. Let the employees participate and be a part of the program from the beginning. Keeping employees involved will pay dividends.

As demonstrated with the football example, it is essential to include the CEO and top decision makers in the process from the beginning. Many companies attempt to launch loyalty programs but fail because the program was not fully embraced, planned, or thought through at each level of the organization.

A loyalty program needs to be:

Planned

Diagrammed

Mapped

Designed

Outlined

Drafted

Written

Practiced

Tested

The impact of being prepared or not being prepared, of having complete company buy-in from the top down, can go much beyond you as an individual. If you are not prepared, the trickle-down effect can be very costly to your company and time-consuming to others involved, including potential vendors and/or suppliers.

I've had the opportunity and privilege over the years to meet and talk with dozens upon dozens of companies, large and small, preparing to launch a customer loyalty initiative. My job is to make sure they are well-informed and well-prepared. If you are launching a loyalty program for your company, your job is to make sure everyone involved is well-informed and well-prepared.

Here are some real-life examples to demonstrate the importance of being prepared and having buy-in from the CEO as you contemplate your loyalty strategy. Your preparedness will be an asset to your company and can positively affect others who will contribute to your effort.

Ensure the CEO Is On Board

I received a phone call from a *Fortune* 500 company with more than 1,000 retail locations about launching a loyalty program. The company was a natural fit and perfectly aligned and structured to begin a customer loyalty program. It made a substantial investment into upgrading its point-of-sale (POS) systems across all locations (which was the key factor to enable a loyalty program).

On the initial call, the woman heading up the project said the company was very committed to launching a loyalty program and needed assistance from me mapping out the program identity. The first question I asked her was if there was complete company buy-in, from the CEO down. She said there was complete buy-in and noted she wouldn't waste my time otherwise.

Over the course of the next several months, including three in-person visits, six pricing proposals, and the loss of more than 500 hair follicles, she informed me that she needed to get buy-in from the president of her division and overall approval of the loyalty program strategy.

That's when I knew there was trouble. For the first time, I realized middle management was making decisions without first consulting with the division president. After they talked to the president they came back and said that due to a change in strategy and overall timing, the company had made a decision not to launch a loyalty program. I felt as though I was hit in the gut.

If you've ever been in a similar situation, you understand the feeling. It is one of those life lessons that change you forever. So, shame on me for not talking directly to the decision maker, and shame on her for not respecting my worth. Rest assured, the same mistake will not happen again.

In hindsight, the entire process could have been avoided and the time, resources, and expense could have been put to better use elsewhere.

TAKEAWAY: GET A COMMITMENT AND A SIGNATURE FROM THE DECISION MAKER!

Be Prepared

At a trade show, we met a midsize retailer that needed assistance with its complete loyalty strategy. The company had spent the previous two years doing research and was now ready to carry out its loyalty plan. Before we entered into a discovery agreement, we requested a call with the CEO and team to ensure there was complete company buy-in. To my delight, there was. The CEO gave his blessing and designated the team in charge to carry out the mission.

Upon signing the agreement, we worked together to outline the goals of the loyalty program and all of the steps that were needed to launch a successful program. We assigned an owner to each one of the tasks on our checklist and held weekly conference calls to ensure a successful launch.

One by one, the objectives were met, and the program went into a live test mode. Selected employees tested the program over a two-week period and last-minute kinks were ironed out before the official launch. When the program finally launched, all of those involved were pleased with the smooth transition from test mode to the live launch. Its team was ready, prepared, equipped, and organized.

Being prepared affords the opportunity to put focus back on the customer.

Internal Affairs

Oftentimes there are internal struggles as to what the right direction for the company should be when considering a loyalty program. As each of you define your own definition of loyalty, it is helpful to first define what the objective of a loyalty program will mean for your company.

The retailer in the next example is a family-owned company and ownership is split 50/50 between the father and son. The father had successfully operated the business for more than 30 years, and the son was beginning to take over more of the day-to-day responsibilities. Although the program eventually launched without a hitch, there were some struggles leading up to making the decision to launch a loyalty program.

The son was very interested in initiating a loyalty program for the company's most loyal customers. The father wanted nothing to do with it.

The son was convinced that initiating a program would better position the company over its competitors. The father disagreed.

The son conducted his own research and found that loyal customers can be up to 100 percent more profitable than a nonloyal customer. The father said that was nonsense.

The son needed his father's consent to make a capital investment to launch the program, and was highly confident the investment would come back as a multiple in return. The father said, "Forget about it."

In the end, the son won the father over, but it wasn't easy. The son was passionate about his direction. He was proactive, willing to take risk, and motivated to put together the most successful loyalty program within his market segment. The son wanted to be first to market. The son wanted every one of his loyal customers to carry a plastic card in their wallet with his logo on it. The father showed no interest because he was set in his ways.

In situations such as this, it is crucial that there is a trust factor between all owners and management to drive loyalty program decisions. There will always be differences in opinion when it comes to the way the loyalty program should be designed, or whether it's even the right decision.

If you are the initiator, it's much easier to earn management's trust if you are prepared and ready to demonstrate that the path you want to take is indeed the path that is best for the company and that the team behind the program has the company's best interests in mind. Conduct your research and outline your plan so that your vision can be seen and shared by all those involved.

All successful loyalty programs have complete companywide buy-in. A road map was built, the plan was followed, and the teams put in charge of execution of the loyalty program had complete buy-in from top management.

Most likely, you belong to one or more successful loyalty programs. Here's a list of ten popular and highly successful loyalty programs across a variety of industries. Chances are you're familiar with or may even participate in one or more of the programs listed.

1. CVS/pharmacy ExtraCare®

2. Southwest Rapid Rewards®

3. Dick's Sporting Goods ScoreCard®

4. American Express Membership Rewards®

5. Saks Fifth Avenue SAKSFIRST

6. Kroger® Plus

7. Barnes & Noble Member Program

8. Speedway SuperAmerica Speedy Rewards

9. T.G.I. Friday's® *Give Me More Stripes*™

10. Marriott Rewards®

The loyalty programs on the previous page include representatives from the pharmacy, airline, sporting goods, credit card, department store, supermarket, bookstore, gas and convenience, food service, and hotel industries. Each company is an industry leader that has successfully implemented a loyalty program as part of its overall corporate marketing strategy. Each understands the importance of catering to its loyal following. And each, without a doubt, has buy-in from the top down. Research and study these programs as you build or enhance your own program. Look to these programs to provide you with loyalty program best practices and prompt you with some ideas to better position your own. Look at each of the websites to see how the loyalty program is tied into an overall company strategy.

Joseph Mirabito is the CEO of Mirabito Energy Products in upstate New York. The company owns and operates more than 60 gas and convenience stores and has thousands of home-heat customers, mostly in rural areas. In 2003, Mirabito decided to launch a loyalty program that was made available to all of his customers.

After he consulted with his management team and board of directors, he knew he had to send the right message to his company so employees would understand the importance of the new marketing path they were about to undertake.

What did Joe Mirabito do to get the attention of his team? He pounded on the conference room table with his fist and exclaimed,

"From today forward, Rewards Plus *is* our marketing strategy! Learn it, live it, breathe it—because as of now it's a prerequisite to understand the program inside and out if you want to continue to work for Mirabito Energy."

It worked. Six years later the program is running strong. Joe Mirabito knows all of his top customers by name, where they live, and how much they spend on home heating or at the convenience stores.

Joe Mirabito will be the first one to admit that before he launched his loyalty program he knew very little about his customers and their buying habits. He was pleasantly surprised to see how often certain segments of customers were transacting after the program launched.

Certified

Certified Savings Program

ABOUT THE PROGRAM: Earn points on gasoline and most store purchases and trade them in for gasoline discounts, gift cards, or free merchandise. In addition, you'll earn a 2-cents-per-gallon discount on every gas purchase by activating your card for ACH payment (funds are transferred from your checking account), or if you prefer to pay with cash it knocks off 3 cents per gallon of gas purchased.

WHAT I LIKE: There are rewards for just about every level of spending, both in the store and for fuel. If you are a loyal customer, you will see savings all year long at Certified. This is a very strong program for a regional gas and convenience store chain. If you live in the greater Columbus, Ohio, area you are in luck!

FOR MORE DETAILED INFORMATION VISIT:

certifiedoil.com

STEP 3

GOLDEN TIPS

1. Ensure there is companywide approval to build or enhance your loyalty strategy, including acceptance and complete buy-in from the top kahuna.

2. Align all company resources so that each department participates in, and is part of, your overall strategy.

3. Prepare a complete blueprint of the program, and use it as your handbook and guide.

4. Circulate information to your employees once you make your decision to launch. Get them involved and keep them informed!

5. Conduct research on existing loyalty programs to gain insight and ideas for your own loyalty strategy.

CREATE AFFINITY: A Desire for Your Product, Brand, or Service

WHAT DO YOUR EXPERIENCES have to do with your affinity toward a company, brand, product, or service? **Just about everything!** Each experience customers have is a microcosm of the overall value and confidence they place in your brand. With each interaction, they subconsciously rate the experience until they formulate their favorable expectation of your business in their mind. This decision reflects the level of confidence or affinity they have toward the brand, which in turn influences future purchasing decisions.

Customers tend to approach purchasing as they would a stoplight, and their decision process often has a similar effect. If they are feeling good about the experience, they will proceed as they would approach a green light, with high confidence. If there are deterrents, the customer will yield with caution as if the stoplight were turning yellow. Any unpleasant situation typically has the same effect as if the stoplight is red. Customers will stop in their tracks and avoid making a purchase at all costs. **Negative experiences put consumers in *stop* mode.**

Essential Step 4: CREATE AFFINITY: A Desire for Your Product, Brand, or Service

Consumers tend to have resolve and hold true to their purchasing convictions, but a natural reaction is for consumers to give a business a second chance. Consumers are forgiving, and will normally attempt to have positive experiences before writing the business off entirely.

That's why you see companies such as Nordstrom work so hard to please their customers with each and every interaction. Nordstrom is proactive and wants to foster positive experiences. It recognizes the better it treats its customers, the more loyal those customers will be.

Nordstrom is all about customer loyalty and brand affinity. Nordstrom understands that because you pay for quality, you deserve quality treatment in return. As with Starbucks Coffee, Nordstrom also strives to make each customer experience a memorable one. Each positive experience reinforces the Nordstrom brand and your affinity to its brand always remains top of mind.

Nordstrom has mastered combining a personal touch with offering high-quality products and exemplary service.

Going the extra mile will pay long-term dividends toward building affinity and overall customer loyalty to your brand.

Nordstrom recognizes its customers are sophisticated shoppers and treats them as such. It recognizes the positive reaction that comes from walking around the counter to hand the customer his shopping bag. It recognizes that all of the intense training it provides its associates comes back tenfold to the business. Nordstrom is living proof that there's no such thing as treating a customer *too* well.

I received a few Nordstrom gift cards for my birthday and thought I would treat myself to a nice pair of shoes. I tried on several pairs and settled on a pair of black Bruno Magli driving shoes. Nordstrom was having its half-yearly sale, so I only had to pay about $30 out of pocket after using the gift cards. In less than a week I received a handwritten thank-you letter in the mail from Bryan, the sales associate. The card read:

For the cost of the paper and a 44-cent stamp, Bryan the sales associate and Nordstrom the company performed a small but important task, which is an investment in their customers. The card alone will strengthen my connection to Nordstrom and will solidify the bond I have with it as a consumer.

The **4th ESSENTIAL STEP** to Build a Successful Customer Loyalty Strategy is to **CREATE AFFINITY**. As you piece together all of the relevant ingredients of customer loyalty, creating affinity emerges as an important part of the complete package. Creating affinity is important in bringing top-of-mind awareness to your brand and in imbedding a positive image in your customers' minds so they think of your business first when it's time to make a purchase decision. Your employees should be constantly reminded that going the extra mile will pay long-term dividends toward fostering affinity and overall customer loyalty to your brand.

So how do you *create affinity* with your customers? It is done through genuine dedication to pleasing your customers. Creating affinity is the culmination of everything good you can do for a customer.

Creating affinity means:

- Greeting customers upon first contact.

- Going out of your way for customers.

- Staying late for customers.

- Doing research to find a specific product for customers.

- Carrying a new product when requested.

- Accepting returns.

- Knowing customers by name.

- Listening to customers.

- Communicating to customers.

- Holding the door for a customer.

- Smiling.

Creating affinity is thanking customers for their business, each and every purchase!

Creating affinity is the culmination of everything good you can do for a customer.

Creating affinity is going the extra mile so your customers recognize you care and appreciate their business. Affinity is building a bond with your customers so they feel part of your brand and can identify personally with your business. **Affinity is creating a positive link with customers so they become repeat buyers.**

I typically travel about 150 days each year. While traveling, I pay close attention to how well companies build affinity with their customers. I observe how well I'm treated by attendants and how well other customers are treated. As with most people who frequently travel, I have had positive and negative experiences, be it at the airport, car rental desk, hotel, restaurant, or gas station. Each experience has a direct effect on purchasing behavior and the purchasing decisions people continually make.

Avis *Does* Try Harder!

Avis is living proof of a company that practices what it preaches and lives by its company motto. The Avis motto is: "We Try Harder." Avis does try harder. I cannot count the number of times Avis has tried harder for me.

One of the most memorable experiences I've had with Avis happened in 2008. I left a trade show at the McCormick Place in downtown Chicago, quickly stopped to refuel my rental car, and arrived at the Avis rental car return with only an hour before my flight was scheduled to depart. A gentleman named Leroy greeted me when I pulled up. I told him I was running late for my flight.

Within seconds he radioed for another Avis employee to pick me up and asked him to drive me directly to the terminal so I didn't have to wait around for the shuttle. I checked in 45 minutes prior to my departure and easily made my flight. Leroy demonstrated to me that Avis does indeed try harder and provided further assurance that my affinity is to the Avis brand.

That experience and many other positive experiences with Avis make them my top choice when renting a car. My positive experiences with Avis built my overall affinity toward their brand, and it was all the little things they did that make them my first choice.

Be like Avis—
Try Harder

To Affinity and Beyond!

The year 2007 was one of the worst in history for air travel. After several incidents played out in the media (massive delays, tremendous increases in delayed and lost luggage, and unacceptable customer service levels at the counter and in the planes themselves), the airlines publicized that they would be improving customer satisfaction significantly in 2008. I was anxious to take my first flight in 2008.

On January 3, 2008, I took a Northwest Airlines flight from Binghamton, New York, to San Antonio, Texas, with a scheduled 90-minute layover in Detroit. I was traveling with our company CEO, and we were meeting our company CTO in Detroit. The plan was to meet in the Detroit terminal and fly together to San Antonio. Our meeting was with a large oil company that had an interest in launching a customer loyalty program.

The plane departed on time and landed in Detroit at 6:30 P.M., and our connecting flight was scheduled for 7:55 P.M. Everything appeared normal until the pilot made a relatively slow approach and a sudden stop about 100 yards from the gate. He announced that there would be a five-minute delay until the ground crew arrived. Five minutes turned into 10, which turned into 20, then 40. By this time, people on the plane were getting agitated because many had connecting flights.

We knew that the chances of making our connecting flight were lessening by the minute. We began to make phone calls to see what other alternatives were available to get to San Antonio that night or early the next morning.

Our CTO was awaiting our arrival at the departure gate for the San Antonio flight. I called him every 10 minutes to give him updates from the plane, and he was relaying the messages to the attendants at check-in. All were on board for the San Antonio flight as he pleaded with two attendants at the counter to hold the plane for us. He was unfortunately turned down, and was asked to go to customer service to look for other options. After waiting nearly 90 minutes on my plane (the same length of time between our arrival and the time our connecting flight was scheduled to depart), the ground crew arrived and the plane was cleared to proceed to the gate.

As we deplaned, a customer service representative was making an announcement that all passengers connecting to San Antonio needed to proceed to Gate A–55 immediately. I was baffled. I had just talked with my co-worker who told me the plane departed. I called his cell phone and in amazement he told me the same information as the attendant at the gate. The plane had just turned around, and it was going to wait for us to board.

It took about ten minutes for us to jog from Gate C–34 to Gate A–55. The entire time I was in disbelief. Why would the plane be waiting? Why had it turned back to the gate after it already left? We couldn't wait to get to the gate.

As we approached Gate A–55, the attendants began to clap, and the pilot was at the door waiting. We quickly gave our ticket stubs and were hurried on to the plane as the pilot walked behind us. "Lucky, lucky, lucky," he shouted. "Today is your lucky day. In all of my 18 years as a pilot I have *never* witnessed this. They wouldn't bring a plane back to the gate for the president," he added.

It turned out that the supervisor at the customer service counter wanted to send a message. Apparently the Detroit ground crew had a less than satisfactory track record for meeting and unloading incoming planes. The supervisor told my co-worker that she had the plane turned around to prove a point. After numerous complaints from people missing their connecting flights and the airline's commitment to start out the New Year right, the supervisor said, "Enough is enough."

We were fortunate that night, but dozens of other passengers were not. I now have affinity toward Northwest Airlines for turning a negative experience into a positive experience. The key is to give your best effort to each and every customer, every single time.

Customer satisfaction, devotion, allegiance, reliability, dependability, and commitment all play into customer decisions when they decide to do business with you and, even more importantly, when they decide to continue to do business with you.

Airlines, hotels, retail stores, and supermarkets are all aware that customers have affinity toward specific brands. Many of these national brands understand *The Power of Loyalty* and understand that increasing a customer's affinity is a large part of their overall loyalty strategy.

Affinity Cards

One of the ways loyalty marketers have created customer affinity is through the issuance of an affinity credit card or loyalty card. Airlines, grocers, and rental car companies all provide their customers with loyalty cards as a way to identify them, maintain their business, and cultivate affinity to their brand. Credit card issuers have followed suit. The thought is to motivate the customer to carry your card and to provide them benefits for their repeat business. Every company is aiming for the affinity card cliché: **OBTAIN TOP OF WALLET STATUS**. And it worked. Consumers are hooked on "affinity programs," which are in essence loyalty programs. They want to accumulate the rewards currency of choice so they can one day earn the free airline ticket, hotel stay, or Bose® Wave® music system. Affinity cards provide customers with a small piece of ownership in your brand.

Companies such as MBNA (acquired by Bank of America in 2005) have mastered the customer affinity experience through issuing co-branded credit cards. MBNA was the largest independent credit card issuer, specializing in affinity-type cards. MBNA began issuing credit cards for many national associations, including the American Dental Association, Sierra Club, and the National Education Association.

It continued to add various college alumni associations, and eventually added professional and collegiate sports teams to its portfolio. MBNA positioned itself as an industry leader and relied on its partners to promote the cards to their members and die-hard fans. An emotional tie to a brand can be an effective way to build affinity.

Want to create brand affinity for less than $100? Go to thepowerofloyalty.com/yourbrand and I will promote your brand through my network.

How can you emotionally tie your customers to your product or service? Strategize about how you can effectively make connections with your customers' emotions. Schools, sports teams, colleges, church groups, charities, hospitals, and unions: Every consumer has emotional ties to something. It's your job to figure out what these are.

There are dozens of companies I have watched over the years that do an exceptional job building customer affinity. This book is not big enough to showcase them all, but here's a list of my Top 20:

1. American Express®
2. Apple®
3. Avis®
4. Barnes & Noble
5. Bloomingdales
6. eBay®
7. FedEx Office℠
8. Lowe's®
9. Marriott®
10. Bank of America®
11. NASCAR®
12. Neiman Marcus
13. Nordstrom
14. Panera Bread®
15. Saks Fifth Avenue
16. Sam's Club®
17. Southwest Airlines®
18. Starbucks®
19. Visa® Signature
20. Zappos.com

Not surprisingly, many of these companies also have exceptional loyalty programs. Good companies understand the importance of building customer affinity into their overall loyalty marketing plan.

Enlighten your employees about the positive influence they can have when they create memorable customer experiences. Build upon all the good things you are doing today to create customer affinity toward your company and brand.

Be Humble

But how can I be humble if I'm trying to bury my competition? It's simple. There's no room for arrogance when you're trying to build your company's loyalty and affinity with your customers. It goes against everything you're doing to cultivate an environment that bleeds loyalty. Bear in mind that customers are most attracted to companies that reward them for their patronage and go the extra mile to satisfy their needs. Teach your employees the value of humility. Your employees are being paid to SERVE your customers, and while on your clock, they should passionately embrace your loyalty strategy.

Humility signifies being:

Modest

Unassuming

Respectful

Considerate

"IT IS IN GIVING THAT WE RECEIVE."

—Author Unknown

You don't have to give away the farm, but giving back to your customers is a large part of adopting a successful loyalty strategy. Start thinking early on how you can give back. There are tangible and non-tangible means by which you can give back to your loyal customers. Below list some of the ways you can give back to your customers.

STEP 4

GOLDEN TIPS

1. Customers approach your business as they would a stoplight. Make sure the light is always green.

2. Create affinity by going the extra mile for each and every customer.

3. Loyalty cards are affinity cards and a perfect way to give customers some ownership in your brand.

4. Create memorable customer experiences to enrich customer affinity.

5. The more you give to your customers, the more loyalty you'll receive in return.

NORDSTROM

Nordstrom Fashion Rewards®

ABOUT THE PROGRAM: To participate in Nordstrom Fashion Rewards you must be a Nordstrom credit card or Nordstrom MOD® (debit) cardholder. Once you are a cardholder, the benefits you receive are based on your annual net purchases with your Nordstrom card at Nordstrom, Nordstrom Rack, nordstrom.com and through Nordstrom catalogs. Cardholders on the standard program earn 2 rewards points per net dollar spent. When they accumulate 2,000 rewards points they will receive a $20 Nordstrom Note in the mail redeemable for any merchandise or services in Nordstrom stores, online, and through the catalogs.

WHAT I LIKE: Nordstrom Fashion Rewards is a four-level program, meaning the more the customer spends on their Nordstrom card at Nordstrom, the more benefits they can earn, such as complimentary standard shipping and alterations as well as special inside access. And no matter what level you're at, you'll earn rewards points toward Nordstrom Notes with every purchase on your Nordstrom card.

FOR MORE DETAILED INFORMATION VISIT:
nordstromfashionrewards.com

Nordstrom cards issued by Nordstrom fsb, d/b/a Nordstrom Bank; subject to approval.

Roger L. Brooks

Initiate
Next-Generation
Marketing:
LOYALTY
MARKETING

IT'S A NEW AGE. It's a new era. It's truly a new generation for marketing. Today's technology is swift, and the amount of data you have available to analyze customer behavior is abundant. There is no disputing that it's how you use the data and then market to your customers that will drive you ahead of your competition.

Brace yourself. If you are an old-school marketer and don't have any intention of refining or improving your current marketing strategy as you implement your new loyalty strategy, you can stop reading now.

Next-generation loyalty marketers are innovative, open-minded, and are constantly striving to improve, enhance, and advance their marketing strategy. Loyalty marketing pioneers are emerging from the new marketing world we live in, and due to advancements in technology, marketing objectives are becoming more measurable and meaningful. Many of the loyalty marketers today have had experience working for companies that have embraced loyalty as a means of increasing profitability with top tier customers. As loyalty marketing continues to evolve, marketers must stay on the cutting edge.

- Loyalty Marketing is a new mind-set.

- Loyalty Marketing is new age.

- Loyalty Marketing is open-mindedness.

- Loyalty Marketing is a new way of communicating to your customers.

- Loyalty Marketing is a new way of retaining customers.

- Loyalty Marketing is maintaining your good marketing judgment while embracing the latest technology.

- Loyalty Marketing is utilizing new tools to talk to your customers as you were never able to before.

- Loyalty Marketing is raising the sophistication level of your marketing strategy.

- Loyalty Marketing is a philosophical change in the way you carry out your marketing agenda.

Marketing your loyalty program strategy is a different animal. It is far different than the traditional marketing methods you may be used to. Traditional marketing talks to the masses. Loyalty marketing talks to the individual. Loyalty marketing reaches a customer who has shown interest in your strategy and is willing to allow you access into his world in exchange for a reward for his patronage. Customers who enroll in loyalty programs are willing to receive communications based on their purchasing activity, knowing they will receive a reward in return.

Utilizing Loyalty Marketing means you:

- *Trust the concept.*

- *Embrace the strategy.*

- *Will realize ROI in multiple ways.*

- *Gain access to your most valued customers.*

- *Are marketing something of relevance.*

When you enter the loyalty arena, you're entering the new age of marketing.

The 5th ESSENTIAL STEP to Build a Successful Customer Loyalty Strategy is to INITIATE NEXT-GENERATION MARKETING: LOYALTY MARKETING.

Open-Mindedness

How important is it for your marketing team to be open-minded about loyalty? Uh, VERY!

When it comes to your loyalty program strategy, you can have all of the technology and analytical sophistication in the world; however, if your marketing team is set in its ways and is not willing to take the time to learn and understand the strategic value of your loyalty marketing strategy, you can kiss the success of your program goodbye.

As a loyalty marketer, it is difficult to sit on the sidelines while individuals within your company discourage or disrupt the loyalty marketing strategy.

What are the reasons marketing executives have a difficult time embracing loyalty marketing? Often they are intimidated by the learning curve or are simply comfortable with the current marketing structure. Sometimes they are even intimidated by ruffling the feathers of their co-workers as they try to sell the new concept. Loyalty marketing is not intimidating unless you make it intimidating.

It's quite the contrary. Loyalty marketing is exciting and addicting once it is embraced and understood. Many marketing executives are more concerned with their current workload and are more caught up in their personal gain than adopting proven concepts to increase gross profits.

Hey Rocco! Flip the switch from Traditional Marketing to Loyalty Marketing, would you?

It's not that easy. Making the switch from traditional marketing to loyalty marketing is a process in itself. Although I believe there is no foolproof way to make the switch, the best way is to do it systematically, methodically, and gradually. The switch from traditional marketing to loyalty marketing often resembles the implementation of the loyalty strategy itself. It is a slow and steady process before rolling it out companywide.

I urge any company, large or small, to test its loyalty marketing strategy as a beta before rolling it out to its entire customer base. I highly encourage conducting a pilot program to an isolated geographical group or segmented group by spending tier. It's good to iron out the wrinkles early on in the process.

In the end, it's ALL about the marketing.

Generational Gap?

OK, I will discuss this delicately and first provide you with an example I think you can easily relate to.

Phonograph» Turntable» Record Player» 8 Track» Cassette» CD Player» Satellite Radio» MP3» iPod.

Before consumers became proficient with each new technology, there was a learning curve associated with that proficiency. With each improvement in technology came a new level of learning and sophistication necessary to operate the way music was played. If consumers didn't take the time to learn and understand how to operate the next generation of technology, then they could not listen to music at their leisure. Therefore, they only had two choices: 1) learn how to operate the new technology, or 2) find someone to operate it for them. Otherwise, they couldn't play their music.

The same analogy applies to next-generation loyalty marketing. If loyalty is embraced by your company, then your marketing director has two choices. Embrace the new-age marketing methods, or step aside to let someone else run the show. Keeping an old-school marketer in charge of running your loyalty program is equivalent to trying to download songs from an old phonograph to your iPod. It just won't work.

So who do you put in charge of marketing your loyalty program? The best advice I can give is to find the most open-minded member of your marketing team to lead the way. You'll need a team member who is willing to learn and embrace the new strategy. You may even want to take on this role yourself, at least initially, in order to properly set the stage for your company.

Get in the Groove

I am a student of loyalty marketing. Loyalty marketing is constantly evolving. Loyalty marketing is keeping up with the latest technologies and marketing trends to be able to reach your most loyal customers in the most efficient fashion. Every day I aim to learn from new and existing loyalty programs and see how they are being marketed. I receive dozens of Google Alerts each day, I read industry publications, and I constantly initiate real-life experiences. There isn't any "textbook" way to market your program, so learn from others and adopt your own plan.

Go to thepoweofloyalty.com, and type in "LOYALTY MARKETING" in the search bar to get a list of helpful tips.

The technology of today and what is available to successfully market to loyal customers transcend age and generation. Marketing to loyal customers takes the skill set of a marketer who can effectively embrace the loyalty strategy and carry that strategy through.

It takes a loyalty marketer who can facilitate new marketing methods and successfully market through new channels as well as proven channels. Don't be afraid to market through e-mail, SMS text, and statement and receipt messaging. Loyalty marketers are also finding ways to reach a new generation of customers through various types of social networking such as Facebook, LinkedIn, Twitter, and

YouTube. Start engaging in social networking if you haven't already. The digital age is here, and there are many new ways to market to your customers through various digital and social media.

Loyalty Marketing Exercise

Try doing something new! Place a 2D barcode within an upcoming advertisement to reach a new segment of customers. The 2D barcode can be a video or a link to a website message giving customers insight into a new product or service. Your customers will be intrigued, and you may be surprised with the results and feedback you receive. Most importantly, the test can be tracked 100 percent.

Go to thepoweroflyalty.com, and type in "2D BARCODE" in the search box for more information on this emerging technology.

It is common for small-business owners to take charge and oversee the marketing effort of their loyalty strategy to ensure it succeeds. Business owners know that a dedicated effort is necessary for success. Therefore, I urge you to recruit someone who is deeply passionate, with an owner mentality, to oversee the marketing efforts of your loyalty strategy.

Loyalty programs are typically embraced along with a new-age marketing mind-set, including a next-generation marketing strategy. Here are TWELVE ideas to consider while building your loyalty program marketing strategy.

1. **Find your internal champion to lead the charge.** Do yourself a favor and put a competent, motivated, and

open-minded person in charge of leading your initiative.

2. **Repurpose all or part of your existing marketing budget to operate your loyalty program.** Your program should not become an additional cost center; rather it should be a shift or repurpose of your existing marketing dollars.

3. **Identify your customers and enroll them into your program.** You'll want and need to identify each and every customer enrolled into the program in order to talk directly to them to service their needs.

4. **Obtain all contact information at the time of enrollment, including e-mail address and cell phone.** Ongoing communication to your customers is a key component to any loyalty strategy.

5. **Disengage from absolute discounts.** Providing discounts to the general public encourages price tag shopping for consumers and price wars for competitors. Discounts are only as good as your next price reduction. Only offer discounts to loyal customers who can be identified or that you can segment and market a special offer directly to.

6. **Provide attractive perks to encourage continual use of the loyalty card.** Provide incentives such as issuing points for every purchase, and enter loyal customers into sweepstakes and generate random rewards.

7. **Offer attractive redemption options.** The redemption options should be attractive for all customers. There should be redemption options that are easy to attain, and others that have a "Wow Factor" and are only achievable over time.

8. **Track every transaction completed with the loyalty card.** In order to systematically operate a successful loyalty program, each and every transaction must be tracked.

9. **Analyze purchase behavior and begin to segment customers into different spending buckets.** As the program matures, so should your approach to analyzing behavior so that you can then market offers that are relevant to the audience.

10. **Create target bonus promotions, which are structured to change purchase behavior.** This is accomplished by offering bonus promotions that will motivate customers to earn more rewards currency in order to reach attractive redemption thresholds.

11. **Measure success and ROI down to a loyalty promotion level and repeat successful campaigns.** Each promotion you offer should be measured for effectiveness.

12. **Encourage participation from vendors and suppliers to offset a portion of the cost of your loyalty program and/or have specific loyalty promotions promoting their product.** Don't try to underwrite your entire program. Talk to the companies that you support every day and ask them to participate in your loyalty program.

Use your existing marketing budget. I'm often asked, "How much will it cost to market the loyalty program?" Or, "What will my ROI be for my loyalty initiative?"

My response—what a joke!

What ROI did you receive on the new POS system you installed?

What ROI did you receive on the upgrade of your ISP?

What ROI did you receive on the billboard ad?

What ROI did you receive on the automatic doors you installed?

What ROI did you receive on your new company logo?

What ROI did you receive since you took out the rotary telephones in your call center?

MOST IMPORTANTLY—What ROI did you receive last year utilizing your existing marketing budget?

Come on, give me a break. Corporate America wastes too much time trying to understand ROI when evaluating the viability of a loyalty strategy instead of trying to better understand the needs of loyal customers. Don't you think high-profile businesses would discontinue their loyalty initiatives if they weren't successful? When was the last time you heard of a business discontinuing its loyalty program? They are few and far between. Many companies have had to refine a loyalty strategy because their programs were too rich to begin with. Many airlines in particular have had to modify their programs in order to remain competitive and decrease their overall exposure and liability. But, by and large, companies are aiming to constantly improve the value proposition of their strategy, not devaluing or discontinuing them.

As a rule of thumb, loyalty programs reward customers 1–3 percent in return of their total spending. This percentage can fluctuate somewhat by industry, but that is the norm. It's what you do with the 1–3 percent that will set you apart from your competitors. Do you give it back to the customer in the form of cash, points, discounts, or rebates? That's where your innovative marketing skills come into play.

Loyalty programs are not a quick and easy fix to mending financial vulnerability. Loyalty programs are a strategic tool to use in conjunction with excellent customer service, innovative ideas, and providing the best possible product/service to your loyal followers.

ROI is obviously important to any business; however, measuring ROI of your loyalty program is not as easy as plugging numbers into a spreadsheet, at least right away. Systematically measuring ROI requires measuring the profitability of your loyal customer's behavior against each loyalty campaign or instance. It will take some time to be able to measure your *true* ROI. All pieces of your loyalty strategy will need to be fully implemented, and you'll need enough history built up to measure it against. You may, however, see some initial results as early as two to three months into the launch as you put the proper tools in place.

Measuring ROI should take into account all expenses incurred, including capital expenditures. When you utilize your existing marketing budget or repurpose a portion of that budget, the loyalty program becomes part of your complete marketing strategy.

If you separate your loyalty budget from your traditional marketing budget, you put yourself at a disadvantage from the start. Try to combine all marketing so there is a clear picture.

Keep in mind, if loyalty programs were easy to implement or inexpensive to maintain, every Tom, Dick, and Harry would have one. The fact of the matter is there are hard costs when executing a program, and there is an ongoing financial commitment to maintain the program. But, if you are smart about your strategy, such as repurposing your existing marketing budget, you can drastically reduce your costs of implementation and ongoing expense. The more organized you are in molding the loyalty strategy into your core business practice, the sooner you will receive a positive ROI from your decision. The idea of implementing loyalty in the first place should be to influence patronage, and your financial exposure should be less expensive to maintain than giving in to customer defection.

Here are TEN important investments you should consider in the preparation and implementation of your loyalty program strategy:

1. Technology and setup costs
2. Employee training
3. Rewards program identifier (loyalty card or equivalent)
4. Enrollment forms
5. Rewards program website
6. Monthly e-statements
7. Rewards program fliers and/or web banners
8. Rewards program advertising and branding
9. Ongoing customer communication (e-mail, text, etc.)
10. Liability of rewards currency (typically 1–3 percent of purchases)

Although implementation is not and should not be as easy as flipping a switch, the message to your customers about reasons for them to enroll should be. The offer to join should be so compelling that the decision to participate is indeed a no-brainer.

In 2005 I had the privilege of meeting and interviewing the late, great Johnny Hart—the creator of the comic strip B.C. If I had one wish before Johnny passed, it would have been to ask Johnny to sketch out a comic strip for me that I could send to all my prospective clients. It would only need to be two frames and would look and read something like this.

Frame 1

Visual: B.C. is looking up reading rules inscribed on a large rock for how to apply for and use a loyalty card.

<u>RULES</u>

Apply for Card.

Use Card.

Use Card Again and Again.

Earn Great Rewards.

Frame 2

Visual: B.C. is scratching his head.

The point being, embracing loyalty can't be that hard to understand, can it? Not even for a caveman.

It works like this:

- Customer has an incentive to be loyal.
- Customer buys from you.
- Company receives more business than before.
- Customer receives their reward.

This is where it all begins. Marketing your loyalty program becomes your new marketing strategy. This is where your shift in mind-set takes place. This is where your creativity and your instincts kick in.

If your strategy includes a loyalty card, use the card itself as a marketing tool. If your customers keep your loyalty card in *top of wallet status* that means you are doing a superb job of marketing use of the card. The more the customer needs to reach for the card, the more value he feels he's receiving.

Many companies are expanding use of their card beyond use with their own brand and are building coalition programs around their overall strategy.

Set-Up a Marketing Calendar

Your marketing calendar should become your loyalty program strategy bible. The calendar should list out every piece of your strategy at least six months in advance. You can always modify your calendar as you go, but the idea is to have a guide in place that you can build upon.

Your marketing calendar should list items such as:

- Important milestones/target dates.
- Monthly promotions.
- Monthly discounts.
- Vendor-specific promotion dates.
- Sweepstake drawings.
- E-mail, other advertising drop dates.

Oh Can-a-da!

How can loyalty marketers in the United States learn from their neighbors when it comes to coalition loyalty? Let me count the ways.

I'm referring specifically to our neighbor to the north, which has slightly more square miles of land, yet is ten times our junior in population. The United States capitalists have typically adopted a generalized philosophy toward our friendly neighbors: "Anything You Can Do, I Can Do Better" (lyrics from the song "Anything You Can Do" from the 1946 Broadway musical, *Annie Get Your Gun*). Canadians would argue, however, that this egotistical philosophy falls short when it comes to their fancies like hockey, maple syrup, and loyalty. Yes, I said, "LOYALTY."

Loyalty programs and coalition programs in particular have thrived in Canada. In this case *coalition* refers to national retail partners (called *sponsors*) who have teamed up to issue a common loyalty program currency. The coalition revolution began in Canada less than 20 years ago when the AIR MILES Reward Program opened its doors and launched a coalition program with anchor partners in virtually all major spending verticals. Today, more than half of Canadian households are active AIR MILES "collectors." In addition, other long-standing loyalty programs such as Aeroplan have evolved and followed suit by developing coalition programs of their own.

So just what is it about coalition programs in Canada and AIR MILES in particular that has the stars aligned perfectly? It comes down to one word—will.

AIR MILES had the will to:

- Issue a nonpayment loyalty card that it calls the "Blue" card.
- Open negotiations and partner with national merchants.
- Overcome point-of-sale and technical challenges.
- Offer category exclusivity.
- Defy the odds of issuing a common loyalty currency.
- Partner with two competing card issuers (American Express and Bank of Montreal).
- Make coalition loyalty happen!

Loyalty marketers in the United States should continue to learn from AIR MILES' success. (It has expanded to Europe and the Middle East.) Now more than ever, the United States is in prime position to offer a common loyalty currency. Reason number one is the current state of the United States economy.

Merchants are in need of any competitive advantage they can get. They are in need of new business opportunities that are compelling, proven, and profitable to their bottom line. Although a majority of leading national consumer giants offers stand-alone loyalty programs, the potential for coalition loyalty in the United States is enormous. The coalition model provides a platform for impactful cross-promotion opportunities as well as tremendous benefits such as the ability to analyze consumer data. The shared data that comes along with coalition loyalty is powerful and, if marketed correctly, has a direct impact on motivating customer behavior. If the incentive is great enough, consumers will change their buying habits.

The beauty of the United States marketplace is there's room for more than one coalition provider. Being first to market is always a key factor, but the reality is the dynamics of the United States marketplace are vastly more complex than in Canada. For example, in the United States, large providers in certain categories such as fuel and grocery tend to be more regionalized. There are many franchise locations in the United States which can create complexities. In addition, payment processing systems and point-of-sale variations can complicate the effort.

That said, there are still enough compelling reasons why coalition loyalty will work. The fact that several category leaders have existing loyalty programs in place today is a big advantage. Currently, there are several companies testing the waters with coalition loyalty in various pockets around the country. There are formal requests for information and proposals circulating around the industry. There are executive-level meetings taking place every day on the subject. There is strategic planning happening in many boardrooms.

It's not a matter of if; rather, it's a matter of when. When will coalition loyalty launch in the United States and what will it look like? It may not look exactly the same in the United States as it does elsewhere, but coalition loyalty can breed success for both sponsors and collectors. But in the end, and as our Canadian neighbors found, this gigantic opportunity will most likely come down to that one small word: the *will* to get it done!

Market Your Redemptions

So what are you marketing anyway? Are you marketing a loyalty program just for the sake of it, or do you have a loyalty marketing strategy that will offer your customers attractive redemption options to keep them coming back? The key word here is *options.* People have different tastes, so providing a variety of redemption options will increase your rate of success in reaching the masses.

Before customers enroll into a loyalty program, they'll want to know what their loyalty will buy them. Is it discounts on their current transactions, a gift certificate to use on future purchases, ongoing free shipping, cash back each month, fuel discounts, or accumulation of points for a future redemption in a catalogue? Whatever redemption options you choose, the value proposition should be front and center for your customers to see.

Reinforce the Message

As part of your loyalty marketing plan, your customers should have constant reinforcement of the program. Any touch point to your customers, including advertisements, should include a mention of the loyalty program.

BMO Bank of Montreal

BMO AIR MILES MasterCard

ABOUT THE PROGRAM: Earn reward miles and pay no annual fee.

- 1 AIR MILES reward mile for every $20 in card purchases.
- 1.5x reward miles on all your card purchases at Shell locations in Canada.
- 1.5x reward miles at National Car Rental and Alamo Rent A Car locations worldwide.
- Up to 25 percent rental discount at National Car Rental and Alamo Rent A Car locations worldwide.
- Triple reward miles at Rewards Plus merchants (participating local merchants).

WHAT I LIKE: BMO cardholders can earn the valuable AIR MILES currency at any merchant that accepts MasterCard, or customers can opt for Cashback rewards. Plus you can earn bonus AIR MILES when you shop at Rewards Plus merchants, including more than 1,500 local merchants participating throughout Canada.

FOR MORE DETAILED INFORMATION VISIT:
bmo.com

STEP 5

GOLDEN TIPS

1. Embrace the new age of marketing called loyalty marketing.

2. Loyalty marketing differs from traditional marketing, and there is clearly a shift in mind-set.

3. In the end, it is all about the marketing.

4. Repurpose your existing marketing budget to accommodate loyalty marketing.

5. Research coalition marketing as a viable component to your strategy.

Identify Your
CUSTOMERS

Being able to identify your customers is the single most important component in building a successful customer loyalty strategy. It is the only way you will be able to gather data and intelligence on a continual basis about your customers' buying habits, and communicate a compelling value proposition efficiently.

There are businesses such as airlines, hotels, rental car companies, and online businesses that already require customers to identify themselves before transacting. The fact that your business may not require you to identify your customers does not give you a free pass on identifying them. You can identify customers in different ways, but the predominant method, especially with formal loyalty programs, is through issuing loyalty cards.

Loyalty cards typically have an imbedded magnetic stripe (magstripe) on the reverse side of the card, sometimes accompanied by a bar code to identify the customer at the POS. Loyalty cards are individually numbered, unique to each customer, and the preferred industry standard identifier. Customers, however, can be recognized through any number of identifiers: a driver's license, a telephone number, an e-mail address, or any account number exclusive to the individual assigned to the card. Loyalty cards are the preferred identifier because they are widely accepted and considered a distinctive marketing tool.

Without a doubt, you've been exposed to a number of loyalty cards over the years. Your first loyalty card was probably from an airline carrier. You next card was most likely from a rental car company, grocer, or hotel chain because these were among the industry pioneers. Loyalty cards are generally issued upon enrollment in order to track all customer purchase activity. There are several marketing benefits from loyalty cards that are outlined later in this chapter.

Need help with sourcing loyalty cards?

Go to thepowerofloyalty.com, and type "Loyalty Cards" in the search box to receive help on sourcing companies that manufacture loyalty cards.

The type of loyalty card you issue is generally based on your type of business. Businesses that do not have a method of reading a magstripe issued card through a POS terminal are at a disadvantage, but may potentially find alternatives through scanning a bar code or entering another unique identifier into the POS, such as a telephone number, if applicable. You may be familiar with alternative identifiers. CVS Pharmacy is one of the industry leaders in the loyalty program space. The CVS ExtraCare® rewards card acts as the loyalty identifier, yet the system is capable of tying transactions to a specific account by using the customer's telephone number listed in her profile. If the customer forgets her card, the associate has backup, and can key in the customer's phone number. Having more than one method of identifying the consumer provides a positive customer experience.

As you'll see later, the importance of selecting the right loyalty software is not only for ID purposes but also for tracking purchases, issuing of relevant rewards, and measuring results of your promotions. You may find that integration with the POS is too costly or not technically feasible and that you may need to look for other options. Keep in mind the importance of protecting your customers' privacy and security. You'll need to investigate the need

Go to thepoweroflloyalty.com, and type "PCI" in the search box for helpful information on data and security.

for PCI Compliance and any potential impact or vulnerability to customer data. Companies such as Trustwave can assist you with questions you may have regarding your data security and customer compliance needs.

Having more than one method to identify customers provides for a more positive customer experience.

Do You Have an Existing Identifier?

If you have an existing card in place, a proprietary card (common in retailing), co-branded credit card, reloadable gift card, or frequent shopper discount card (common in grocery stores), you are in a good position to add loyalty functionality to the card as an add-on benefit. Financial institutions such as banks, credit unions, and credit card issuers are also in perfect position to use an existing payment instrument as the loyalty card.

You can utilize an existing card if it's in place or issue a new card if it's not. Either way, the card will act as the identifying linchpin for your loyalty program.

In retail, the loyalty card is an exclusive identifier that accompanies each transaction in order to capture when, what, and how often your customers are making purchases. The loyalty card is normally a plastic card and is typically identical in structure to a credit or gift card. The technical difference is that the stand-alone loyalty card is typically not used as a payment tender but rather as a means of identifying the customer and connecting his purchase and rewards activity. Many companies commonly utilize a payment card such as an issued or branded credit card, proprietary card, or gift card as the loyalty program identifier. Combining a loyalty card with a payment card has advantages, including loading cash rewards on to the card itself once the customer reaches a threshold.

The most fundamental and essential step with any loyalty program is having the means to identify your customers.

The **6th ESSENTIAL STEP** to Build a Successful Customer Loyalty Strategy is to IDENTIFY YOUR CUSTOMERS. The most fundamental and essential step with any loyalty program is having the means to identify your customers in order to communicate with them and eventually reward them for their repeat business.

How do you get the loyalty cards into the hands of the right people? It's simple: **All customers are the RIGHT customers.** I urge you to get as many cards in to as many hands as possible. The data that you will collect on each customer is worth the cost of the plastic you'll issue. AND, each customer will carry your mini-billboard in his wallet or on her key chain. You will be pleasantly surprised to discover who your loyal customers *actually* are vs. who you *think* they are.

Identifying your customers has invaluable benefit because you'll capture very useful data in the enrollment process and transactional data thereafter.

Here's some valuable information you should capture in the enrollment process: full name, address, home phone, mobile phone, e-mail address, birth date (month/day), household information, income level, number of vehicles, etc.

The most vital pieces of information you should capture during enrollment are the customer's e-mail address and mobile phone number. Having these two pieces of information will be critical in developing cost-effective means of communicating and marketing targeted promotions to your loyal customers. The benefit to you is that marketing to your customers through these methods can be as quick as you need it to be.

Survey Says!

Survey questions are also quite common at the time of enrollment. You'll be able to ask specific questions to help you gain greater insight so you can better run your business and your loyalty program. This data will be beneficial once you begin to segment your customers and communicate directly to them.

What's My Incentive to Enroll?

Every loyalty program has some gold at the end of the rainbow. Companies such as Saks Fifth Avenue offer an annual in-store gift card as the gold for their members. The incentive for customers to enroll and participate in the Saks First program is the issuance of a Saks gift card worth up to 5 percent of annual purchases. Once enrolled, Saks can market directly to you and offer you incentives to purchase products that are relevant to you. Or you may receive an e-mail message to visit Saks within the next ten days to receive bonus rewards on select items.

Like Saks, many major retailers are adopting loyalty programs and rewarding their customers for making purchases using their in-store company-issued credit card, also known as a proprietary credit card. The proprietary card serves as both the loyalty identifier and payment tender.

The Power of Loyalty

You have undoubtedly been offered an incentive to open a charge account at checkout when you've made a retail purchase. "Save an additional 15 percent today when you open a charge account with us." These promotions are often attached to proprietary cards, which can have a loyalty component built into the payment tender. The loyalty program is an added benefit for customers who utilize the card. Many of the major department stores such as Neiman Marcus, Nordstrom, Belk, Dillards, and JCPenney have loyalty programs tied into their proprietary card. The proprietary card acts as the identifier (loyalty card) and payment instrument all in one. Retailers want customers to carry and use their proprietary cards because they build affinity, loyalty, and profit all in one card. There are endless loyalty program promotion opportunities associated with proprietary cards.

Here are **SIX** reasons why Proprietary Cards make perfect Loyalty Cards:

1. The customer identifier is already in place.
2. There is a way to capture payment.
3. There are typically months or years of payment history available.
4. There's an existing means to communicate (through statement messaging, statement inserts, on website or e-mail messaging) to customers.
5. There are line item details available from purchases as a trigger for rewards.
6. There's a compelling need to issue rewards to customers who carry your card.

No Card, No Foul!

If your company does not have a proprietary card or credit card in place, you can issue a standard loyalty card like those issued by many grocers. The loyalty card will typically have one or a combination of the following components as the way to identify customers and capture their information:

- Distinct customer number.
- Bar code.
- Magnetic stripe (mag-stripe).
- Radio frequency identification (RFID) tags.

Determining what method you use to capture information depends on what limitations you have at the loyalty host (technology platform) and/or POS. It is important to have your IT team engaged from the start in the decision-making process as to what mechanism will be used to identify customers.

I Know I Need to Issue a Loyalty Card, but How Does the Enrollment Process Work?

Below are SEVEN important items to remember when issuing loyalty cards:

1. Streamline the enrollment process for your customers. Allow them to enroll in-store (if applicable) or online at their leisure.

2. Have your loyalty cards pre-activated so that customers can begin to use the card at the time of enrollment.

3. Capture all mandatory fields at the time of enrollment.

4. Encourage your associates to ensure all fields are complete and legible. If online, have mandatory field requirements.

5. Offer an initial incentive for customers to enroll; offer a free product or discount.

6. Offer an added incentive for customers to make their first loyalty program purchase.

7. Allow customers to provide a second form of identification as the loyalty identifier, that is, driver's license, phone number, or thumbprint.

Important: Initiate enrollment goals for all those involved with the enrollment process. The more customers you can enroll, the more likely you will be able to identify and eventually market directly to customers. Marketing directly allows you to measure and eventually positively motivate customers' purchasing behavior.

Why doesn't every company have a loyalty program? There are, of course, naysayers who don't believe loyalty programs necessarily work, but it still amazes me the number of companies that don't even have a loyalty strategy on their radar. Keep your eye out, though. You'll begin to see more and more programs emerge in every industry imaginable. It is only natural that as competitors offer a loyalty program, others will follow suit.

Issuing a loyalty card (or equivalent) is the distinguishing factor for identifying your most valuable and profitable customers.

True Story

I received a call from a convenience store operator in Texas who wanted to start a loyalty program. He insisted that the program be implemented without any issuance of a loyalty card and without asking the customer for any type of identifier. He was convinced that he could successfully implement and maintain a loyalty program and reward customers for their purchasing activity without requiring them to identify themselves. He was dead set against issuing a loyalty card. He didn't want to slow down his already busy register lines by asking a customer to enroll in a program or asking for their card before each purchase. I told him that short of installing thumbprint readers or implanting RFID tags under the customer's skin, he would have to issue a loyalty card or at minimum capture the customer's phone number for identification purposes. He opted not to launch a loyalty program because it would "inconvenience" his customers.

The lesson learned with this real-life example is that as of *today*, there is no easy way to enroll customers in a loyalty program without having their cooperation. There has to be some effort on the part of the customer to allow identification of his purchasing behavior. As with all loyalty programs, there is a trade-off. The customer receives rewards for enrolling, participating, and playing the role of a *loyal* customer, but in the end it's a win-win proposition.

But how far-fetched is the concept of rewarding without identifying? Looking ahead as little as five to seven years from now, the concept the convenience store operator relishes is not out of the question. In time, technology will progress so that customers won't have to carry ten different loyalty cards in their wallets, nor have more than a half-dozen key tags on their key ring.

With the increased use of emerging technologies such as RFID tags, retailers and other businesses will be able to identify customers upon arrival and communicate with customers through a registered Personal Digital Assistant (PDA) device or other external device attached to the shopping cart, basket, or mobile phone device. With emergence of RFID, there is always concern about violations of privacy. The RFID tag will be tied to a driver's license or other common identifying instrument that will provide redundancy with payment, identification, and loyalty promotions. Customers will have to willingly participate in RFID loyalty, which may limit enrollment but has the potential to be very effective.

In addition, there are more complex technology initiatives budding, such as neuromarketing. This is a developing field of marketing that studies consumer response to specific marketing stimuli. Researchers are utilizing technologies such as *functional magnetic resonance imaging* (fMRI) to measure changes in brain wave activity. In its most basic form, an fMRI can determine how you feel about a specific product and why you make specific purchasing decisions. In theory, marketers will be able to target promotions to you based on your thoughts—scary!

Until life like *The Jetsons* becomes reality, there's plenty of time to identify customers by way of traditional loyalty identifiers. Although the loyalty card is basic in form, it is the quickest and most cost-effective way to identify customers today.

What Is the Purpose of Capturing Customer Information?

The main purpose of capturing customer information is to be able to properly identify customers and communicate to them. It is a means to stimulate behavior by driving traffic from target groups or communicating directly to specific customer segments at the POS.

Identifying customers enables:

Relevant rewards.

Relevant promotions.

Relevant marketing messages.

A more profitable customer!

Enrollment Strategy

As described earlier, you must have a plan for enrolling customers in your loyalty program. Once you print your loyalty card, customers will not flock to enroll. Enrollment strategies need to be in place to ensure a steady flow of customers into the program on a continual basis. Plan every stage of enrollment including providing incentives, advertising, marketing, training, data entry, and reward offerings.

What Would Motivate You to Enroll in a Loyalty Program?

What incentives can you offer to make it worthwhile for your customers to enroll? IDEAS: a free product, bonus points, an instant discount off a purchase, or a gift card.

What type of advertising will be needed to reach your customers? IDEAS: in-store, online, traditional media (or all three).

How should you market enrollment to your customers? IDEAS: via e-mail, receipt messaging, website, signage, bag inserts, and take-ones.

Other questions to ask:

- What type of training will be needed for your "A TEAM" of associates?
- Who will do the data entry, and how quickly can you enroll customers into the system?

- Will data entry be performed in-house, outsourced, or sent offshore?
- What attractive redemption options are being offered as the main reason to enroll?
- Are there various levels of redemption options set?
- Are there rewards that have a WOW factor?

All of these questions and pointers should be well thought through as you develop your loyalty strategy and enrollment process.

Sir: Would You Like Paper or Plastic?

Just as the grocery store clerk asks every time if you want paper or plastic, there has to be constant reinforcement of asking for the loyalty card.

As part of the training process (especially in any retail setting), associates should ask each customer if he has his rewards card available. Although some may poke fun at this, the ideal outcome is to get the customer to provide his card before the associate can even ask. If the customer forgets, the associate reacts by asking him for his card. Have signage at the POS or provide buttons for your register clerks that say, "Do you have your rewards card today?"

Can You Punch My Card?
(While You're at it, Can You Punch it Twice?)

The more things change, the more they seem to stay the same. It's 2010, and to this day companies continue to use one of the oldest forms of promoting loyalty—punch cards.

I was in Dallas recently and purchased two magazines (*Entrepreneur* and *Wired*). After I paid, the sales associate at HMSHost took out a paper card with the name "Magazine Plus—A frequent buyer program." It was twice the size of a business card. She took out a hole punch and struck number one and two on the card. The rules are printed clearly on the front of the card along with the offer: "Purchase six magazines from a HMSHost newsstand, get the seventh free!" On the reverse side of the card, there are two blank lines under the heading *Customer Name.* Under that it reads: *Name of Complimentary Magazine* and *Magazine Price.*

Great concept, but there seems to be a good deal of manual labor involved, don't you think?

A punch card frequency program is a loyalty program in its own right, BUT punch card programs:

- Do not allow you to identify your customers.
- Do not allow you to communicate to your customers.
- Do not have reliable accounting or reconciliation procedures.
- Leave room for employee fraud and/or human error.

Although manual punch card programs are relatively easy to implement (with little employee training needed), they can become a promotional and financial liability if they are not closely monitored. If this is the only type of loyalty program you can afford to do, it is better than doing nothing at all.

Subway terminated its Sub Club Card rewards program in 2005. Customers earned stamps for each sub they purchased, earning one stamp for a six-inch sub and two stamps for a foot-long sub. Once the customer earned 12 stamps, he received a free six-inch sub, and with 24 stamps he got a foot-long sub. Although the concept was good, the system became too easy to take advantage of. It's no wonder company officials cited counterfeiting as the main reason for terminating the program.

Today, Subway restaurants issue an electronic version of the manual punch card that is swiped at the POS terminal like a credit card. The business model changed, but the main reward stayed intact—earning a free sub. Customers now earn one point for every dollar spent at Subway. A reward of a free six-inch sub is given on the accrual of 50 points and a foot-long upon earning 75 points. If you do the math, the reward is much richer to the consumer with the electronic program, and Subway can reconcile the free sub offers down to the penny.

SUBWAY® Card Rewards Program

ABOUT THE PROGRAM: The SUBWAY® Card Rewards Program replaces the old Sub Club® stamps program. Under the Rewards Card Program, customers earn one (1) point for each $1 spent on SUBWAY® restaurant menu items. The points can then be redeemed for free menu items. Points are rounded up or down to the nearest dollar, prior to sales taxes. You can ask your favorite SUBWAY® restaurant location if it is participating.

Points can be redeemed for the following menu items:

    10 Points = 1 Cookie

    15 Points = 1 Bag of Chips

    20 Points = 21 oz. Drink

    50 Points = Regular 6" Sub or Flatbread

    65 Points = Premium or Double Stacked™ 6" Sub or Flatbread

    75 Points = Regular Footlong™ Sub or Salad

    100 Points = Premium or Double Stacked™ Footlong™ Sub

    ©2010 Doctor's Associates Inc. SUBWAY® is a registered trademark of Doctor's Associates Inc.

WHAT I LIKE: You can start earning rewards right away, and if you decide to accumulate your points, you can earn a free foot-long after spending $75.

FOR MORE DETAILED INFORMATION VISIT: mysubwaycard.com

Don't Forget About Your Employees

Your employees have the potential to be some of your best and most loyal customers. You have a captive audience, and they clearly understand your products and pricing. If you engage your employees in your loyalty program and reward them as well as or better than your top-tier customers, they will become your biggest advocates.

Your Employees:

Can be some of your BEST customers!

Can be your BIGGEST advocates!

Can engage a LARGE friends and family network!

You may be amazed at the percentage of sales your own employees and their friends and family network make up. Again, it's being able to identify your employees as a customer segment and track their purchase behavior.

I'm a Manufacturer . . . What Should I Use as the Loyalty Program Identifier?

You'll have to get creative, but the ideal identifier for a manufacturer or any business that has limited direct access to customers is to drive customers to a website. Once there, customers will enter their e-mail address, which then becomes the loyalty identifier. You'll now have a means of communicating with your customers—even as a manufacturer.

Wegmans

Wegmans Shoppers Club

ABOUT THE PROGRAM: Save every time you shop with Shoppers Club discounts on products throughout the store. Simply present your card, key tag, or phone number at checkout, and you'll receive instant savings! It's going to be one of the most valuable cards in your wallet. Use it to enjoy a variety of check-cashing services, to store "W-Dollars," and to get special discounts and other perks. Check the Wegmans' website for a complete listing of benefits with Shoppers Club Savings.

WHAT I LIKE: Using the Shoppers Club Card has its advantages, and savings can add up quickly if you use your card every time you shop. Wegmans was ranked number three on the FORTUNE magazine's list of the "100 Best Companies to Work For," and employee satisfaction shows in everything it does. The friendliness of the staff, the superb selection of products, and the cleanliness of the stores all contribute to Wegmans' exceptional customer loyalty strategy. Get this—Wegmans makes automated phone calls to customers who have purchased a recalled product using their Shoppers Club card.

FOR MORE DETAILED INFORMATION VISIT:

wegmans.com

STEP 6

GOLDEN TIPS

1. Being able to identify your customers is the first and most important step for any loyalty program.

2. Issuing a loyalty card is typically the most cost-effective way to identify customers.

3. Utilize an existing payment card such as a credit, debit, or proprietary card as the loyalty program identifier when possible.

4. Capture important information such as e-mail address and mobile phone number as a means of communicating with customers once enrolled.

5. At all costs, issue a card that is electronic in nature to prevent fraud and theft of free product.

TRACK Customer Spending Activity Through Each and Every Touchpoint

ONCE YOU HAVE A MECHANISM in place to identify your customers, the natural next step is to monitor and track what your customers are buying by monitoring their purchase behavior. How often are your loyal customers transacting? What are their typical buying habits? What products/services are they most interested in buying? How can you offer incentives to customers to buy complimentary products or those products they normally buy from your competitors?

These are questions you should be asking yourself as a rule of good business practice. The fact that you are specifically positioning a loyalty strategy to identify your most loyal customers and track their spending habits is one sign that you are interested in taking your business to another dimension, a dimension that dives deep beyond the surface of simply selling as much product as you can to customers you typically care very little about. The reasons for initiating a loyalty strategy should be much deeper than wanting to outdo your profits from the previous quarter or topping last year's numbers.

Your reason for tracking purchase behavior should be a genuine one. Visibly, you want to sell more, and tracking becomes a very personal way to connect to every customer based on her likes and her buying habits. Tracking customer activity will afford you the opportunity to market directly to customers in a more sophisticated way. Once the customer sees that promotional marketing messages are relevant to her, she will appreciate that she is not receiving a generic promotion and will be more likely to respond.

As with the punch card example in Essential Step 6, being able to track spending activity is essential in order to put your customers in specific spending tiers and attempt to motivate their behavior accordingly.

The 7th ESSENTIAL STEP to Build a Successful Customer Loyalty Strategy is to TRACK CUSTOMER SPENDING ACTIVITY THROUGH EACH AND EVERY TOUCHPOINT.

So, how exactly do you track customer spending, or other actions you can reward?

Loyalty software applications were developed to track purchase transactions or behavioral actions. If you are a retailer, you should contact your point-of-sale provider, credit card processor, or IT department to research and implement a reliable and stable loyalty tracking software that suits your needs. Remember, this software needs to be compatible with the identifier you put in place (loyalty card, driver's license, manual entry of phone number, e-mail address, etc.). The software should be able to track all transactions in order to compare the behavior of your loyal base compared to your non-loyal base.

The more intelligence you can gather about your customer, the better you can understand how to motivate her behavior!

If you offer a service, you may want to track behavioral activity such as website visits or use of your service, in addition to purchase transactions. If you are a financial institution, for example, there may be a need to track use of services such as Bill Pay, ATM transactions, or use of a PIN-based debit card in addition to total spending.

Need help in tracking behavior? Go to thepowerofloyalty.com, enter "TRACKING SOFTWARE" in the search box. I will provide assistance on sourcing loyalty software providers for your particular initiative.

Depending on the size and scope of your business, there are a variety of software solutions available in the market today. The type of software needed depends in part on the current systems you have in place. For example, if you outsource your entire POS infrastructure (including the compatible software that ties into your back-end office systems, i.e., inventory, accounting, etc.), your loyalty solution software capabilities may be limited to what that vendor can offer. Otherwise, there are many companies that can integrate with your existing systems and set up a "loyalty host" that will become the central technology platform for your loyalty program.

Whatever your direction, your company will probably need to invest in a loyalty platform to provide necessary tracking of your customers' activity. You'll quickly see that just as computers are required to survive in the business world, **a loyalty platform is required to administer a loyalty strategy**.

What Is a Loyalty Host?

The loyalty host is the central nerve and intelligence center for your loyalty program. It is the lifeblood that maintains every aspect of your program and every detail about your customers' purchase activity. Initially, the host is the platform or system of record that is responsible for all things loyalty. Eventually, it will become such an integral part of your business that you won't know how you survived without it.

As you build your own technology to manage your loyalty program or find a partner to provide the solution, pay close attention to the flexibility of the loyalty platform, including the features and functionalities the loyalty host has to offer. Your loyalty program can only be as savvy and as flexible as your underlying technology allows.

As with any technology, there are varying degrees of functionality available within a loyalty host. For example, if you are in a retail business, it may be important to process loyalty transactions at the product or SKU level. This will provide you the flexibility to track customer spending to the lowest common denominator (individual products or SKUs).

Unless you are well underway with the development and design of a proprietary loyalty platform or are currently working with a partner, I suggest you find an experienced and proven loyalty platform provider who specializes in delivering loyalty solutions within your industry. Building your own loyalty platform takes time, money, and resources. Providers of loyalty tracking solutions have spent years developing and enhancing their applications to accommodate a wide range of industries.

Loyalty tracking systems are very similar to credit card processing systems, although one can argue that loyalty systems are more complex due to business rules and logic the platform must take into account for each transaction. Regardless, the loyalty host in essence processes loyalty transactions, and if in real-time, all loyalty promotions are calculated within hundredths of a second to return the appropriate loyalty promotion(s) prior to check-out.

Here are **TWELVE** questions you can ask when researching loyalty host providers.

1. How much flexibility does the platform have?
2. What are the tracking capabilities?
3. Does the platform process transactions in real-time?
4. Can the loyalty platform be fully integrated with my POS system?
5. Can I offer my customers instant benefits once they are identified as loyal customers?
6. Can the system provide individual receipt messaging capabilities based on variable logic?
7. Can I offer unique promotions to my loyal customers based on the contents in their basket?
8. Does the platform have a web component to allow my customers to log into their account and view their history?
9. Do I need additional hardware?

10. Is there a cost per transaction or a monthly fee?

11. Is there any level of support included, or is that an additional cost?

12. Is there a customer service and fulfillment console available for CRSs to access and fulfillment providers to plug into?

What items are typically tracked in the transaction?

Payment Tender (Type)

Frequency of Visits

Total Transaction or Basket Size

Specific Products or SKUs Purchased

Other Behavioral Actions

Tracking these items provides a virtual snapshot of each transaction so program managers can perform various types of analysis and customer segmentation within the loyalty host. For example, a query can be generated to find out the number of customers that pay with cash, spend more than $15, purchase specific high-margin products, but frequent less than once per month. A marketing message can be sent directly to that segment offering an incentive to those customers that shop two times or more per month.

One of the key benefits to tracking is to build up enough purchase history (after having the program in place for 3, 6, 9, or 12 months) in order to offer your customers incentives relevant to them.

The Power of Loyalty

Loyalty tracking systems are also referred to as:

- Loyalty Scoring Engine
- Loyalty Processing Engine
- Loyalty Rewards Software
- Loyalty Rewards Platform

Whatever the name, the outcome is the same—having a new-age technology available to improve the granularity of your business. Your loyalty host will become the command center for your entire loyalty strategy.

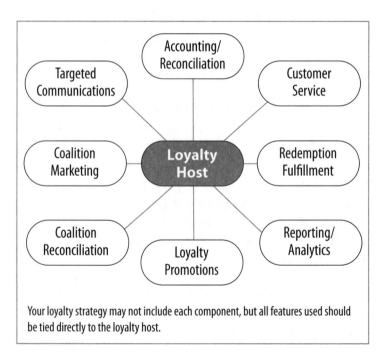

Your loyalty strategy may not include each component, but all features used should be tied directly to the loyalty host.

Your loyalty program will only be as savvy and as flexible as your underlying technology allows.

ExtraCare
CVS/pharmacy®

ABOUT THE PROGRAM: Earn 2 percent back with every purchase in-store and online at CVS/pharmacy; earn one Extra Buck for every two prescriptions purchased in-store and online at CVS/pharmacy (*some exclusions apply*). Every three months your Extra Bucks will print on your store register receipt, or visit CVS.com to print your Extra Bucks. You can also print your coupons before you shop at the ExtraCare Coupon Centers. Spend your Extra Bucks at any CVS/pharmacy location or online the next time you shop! Plus, get instant savings on items featured in its weekly store circular ads, and earn even more Extra Bucks on select brands advertised in its weekly ads.

WHAT I LIKE: If CVS is your primary choice for purchasing prescriptions and other convenient drugstore items, you'll be happy with the return you receive from ExtraCare. In addition, special offers relevant to your historical purchase activity are printed on your receipt.

FOR MORE DETAILED INFORMATION VISIT:
cvs.com

Roger L. Brooks

Lose the Chip

I can't count the number of times I have met with senior level executives who have all of the answers when it comes to implementing a loyalty strategy. Be it an issuing bank, a retailer, or oil company, oftentimes top decision makers make poor decisions throughout their evaluation process when seeking to launch a loyalty program.

Many view the investment in their loyalty platform as a cost center, not as an opportunity to better serve their customers and make them more profitable customers over the long term. If you run the program properly, the loyalty platform and overall loyalty program will serve as your central intelligence office housing an abundance of information about your customer base. Your reason for investing in a loyalty platform in the first place is to better understand customers so that you can better service them over time and keep them loyal forever.

Having a loyalty host in place to track customer spending is simply refining your business. It's an evolution of your technology infrastructure and marketing strategy to outsmart and outhustle your competition. How productive would you be today without a computer? Not very, and that's the point. Your investment in your loyalty platform is a capital expenditure that will provide long-term benefits to your company. For most industries, there's going to come a point when if you're not in the loyalty game in some capacity, you're going to lose.

It's amazing to witness firsthand who loyalty program administrators believe their top customers are vs. who they actually are. I can recall a client who wanted to see a report of his top 100 customers. He wanted to know their name, address, and how much they spent over the course of the calendar year. We ran a query for him and printed the results of the report. He nearly fainted when he saw them. His top 100 customers spent over $1,250,000 that year. He was so flabbergasted with the results that he sent each and every one a $50 fruit basket. For the first time in nearly 75 years of being in business, his company was able to identify its top customers by tracking all of their purchases through the assistance of a loyalty card.

Donald Trump has provided tremendous value to business executives and entrepreneurs alike with his hit TV show *The Apprentice*. Although the reality show is a competition among teams, and eventually individuals, viewers get a firsthand look into what it takes to be loyal to one of the most successful businessmen of our time. You also get insight into what it takes to win at a high level, under strict time restraints. As a participant, you must be on top of your game with every decision you make. You must be loyal to yourself, to your team, and to the cause.

The same holds true for your loyalty platform. The loyalty host is the meat and potatoes of your program. It is the lifeline and your Genie bottle. It will provide tremendous insight and value to your business that you only dream of today. Your loyalty host will grow and mature just like any host that is fed with the proper nourishment.

Tracking Customer Spending Affords

Greater insight into your customers' buying habits.

A complete snapshot of what your customers are buying.

A way to talk to your customers in a one-to-one fashion.

Use Tracking to Your Benefit

If you operate a chain of grocery stores, knowing the exact products your customers purchase has tremendous value. To whom, you may ask?

Answer: To competitive brands.

If 40 percent of your loyalty cardholders currently purchase Coke®, what would it be worth to Coke® to grow that number to 48 percent or 55 percent? Once you are able to identify and track your customers' purchases, that level of data becomes extremely valuable to manufacturers, vendors, suppliers, and payment providers, among others.

Take a shortcut. Go to thepowerofloyalty.com, and enter the words "LOYALTY HOST PROVIDERS" in the search bar. I'll provide you with information about various providers by industry.

If you are a card issuer and have a points program, tracking customer spending at specific merchants can prove beneficial. Once you understand where your customers are transacting, competing merchants will pay for the opportunity to offer cardholders bonus points for a solicited transaction. Simply put, you're paying for a strategic and predictable purchase.

Here are FOUR tips to guide you on your quest to find a loyalty host provider:

1. Contact your existing vendors/suppliers to see if they offer a loyalty solution. Start with your POS provider or payment processor.

2. Contact industry trade associations for provider references.

3. Contact your local chamber of commerce to talk to a community relations specialist.

4. Contact your gift card provider to see if it offers a loyalty solution.

SAKSFIRST

ABOUT THE PROGRAM: If you love Saks, you'll want to be part of this irresistibly rewarding experience. SAKSFIRST spoils you with privileges, preferred service and points that add up to the most coveted reward of all, a year-end SAKSFIRST Gift Card.

Every time you use the classic Saks Fifth Avenue Store Card or the Saks Fifth Avenue World Elite MasterCard® for eligible purchases at Saks, you'll be showered with SAKSFIRST points. And the more you spend, the faster you'll move up the SAKSFIRST tiers, earning more points per dollar and more privileges along the way.

WHAT I LIKE: The rate of return is tied directly to your purchase activity. The more you spend, the more you earn. You must make qualifying purchases; however, Saks frequently offers bonus offers across all categories.

FOR MORE DETAILED INFORMATION VISIT:
saksfirst.com

A sophisticated loyalty host will allow a refined approach for communicating with your loyal customers when it matters most.

Many of the companies that originally brought loyalty platforms to the marketplace are now restricted as the platforms have become outdated. They are restricted in the sense that older systems do not have the flexibility to process loyalty transactions as well as the next-generation platforms do.

Here are features you'll want to consider having available in your platform:

- Points/currency scoring engine
- E-mail/SMS text capabilities
- Capacity to generate monthly activity statements/e-statements
- Customer service interface
- Administrator interface
- Redemption catalog plug-in
- Rewards website plug-in
- Rewards fulfillment tool
- Reporting engine
- Customer segmentation feature
- Promotional setup area
- Customer interface via website
- Accommodate uploads of location/product hierarchy
- Capability to log notes

More recent loyalty platforms (built within the past ten years) tend to offer more features and functionality for running promotions including:

- Time of day
- Day of week
- Type of product (SKU)
- Accumulative promotions
- Frequency of visits
- Total dollars spent
- Combination purchases
- Payment tender

Operating a loyalty program is like playing a chess game. The benefit of your current move may not be realized until later in the game.

STEP 7

GOLDEN TIPS

1. Tracking customer spending provides you with greater intelligence about your customers.

2. Your loyalty systems will play a key role in your ability to repurpose your data.

3. Any investment made in your loyalty strategy is a direct investment in bettering your business.

4. Tracking spending allows you to talk to your customers in one-to-one fashion.

5. Do your homework in finding the loyalty host provider that's best for you.

Motivate Behavior to BENEFIT Customer Relations and Your Profit Margin

M OTIVATE, MOTIVATE, MOTIVATE! This is where it gets fun—the art of changing customer behavior. There are believers and nonbelievers on the possibility of being able to motivate customer behavior. So if you're starting to believe, keep on reading!

It's instinctive and it's human nature. The best way to motivate customer behavior is to provide an incentive or reward for that motivation. Rewarding your customers for performing a specific purchasing behavior is not much different than training your pup to take an action that you want him to take. With enough repetition, your pup can be motivated to react upon instruction if there is a treat or reward for him in the end. Simply put, the pup knows if he follows your command, he'll receive his reward.

Human nature is not much different. People can be motivated to take specific actions that accomplish their internal buying goals, which will in turn accomplish your goals to increase their spending, frequency of visits, or combination purchases (or comparable goals relevant to your line of business). Once more, the way you motivate your customers is dependent of your industry. Now that you are identifying customers and tracking their spending habits, you can motivate them by offering promotions that are relevant and meaningful. Your customers are more likely to respond to a promotion that is relevant to their historical activity.

How do you motivate behavior? Below are FIVE ideas to get you thinking:

1. Offer soft benefits that provide value such as special access limited only to members.
2. Offer relevant promotions through various lines of communication, for example: e-mail, SMS text, receipt messages, statement inserts, rss feeds, Twitter, Facebook, etc.
3. Upsell complementary products/services at the associate level.
4. Keep your strategy fresh and exciting. Offer sweepstakes, random rewards, or special offers for a very limited time frame.
5. Strategically place signage/messaging/web banners that will trigger motivating actions.

Motivate, but Don't Mislead

Once you decide how you'll motivate, always do so in an honorable way. Your customers won't want to be misled into thinking they will receive something greater in value than they actually receive as the reward.

"You may fool all the people some of the time, you can even fool some of the people all of the time, but you cannot fool all of the people all the time."

—Abraham Lincoln

Abraham Lincoln put it best when he said, "You may fool all the people some of the time, you can even fool some of the people all of the time, but you cannot fool all the people all the time."

Of course, the statement was made some 150 years ago and Lincoln was referring to politicians attempting to fool their constituents; however, the quote resonates with me every time I see a program that offers *empty loyalty*. Programs do exist that don't follow industry best practices. Such programs offer an elaborate program on the outside that is only a façade to increase business. In time, savvy customers see through it. Your promotional strategy to motivate behavior must be phony proof. Once your customers lift the hood and kick the tires, the promotions must stand on their own and offer real value, not empty promises.

"Look man, I ain't fallin' for no banana in my tailpipe!"

—Eddie Murphy as Axel Foley in *Beverly Hills Cop*

Remember, whatever you do, don't try to fool the customer! Loyal customers will catch on if the loyalty program does not have true value. This can also backfire and cause customer disloyalty, defeating the entire purpose of implementing your strategy in the first place.

Here are THREE reasons why your rewards offerings should be upstanding:

1. Rewards should be a genuine offering and a sincere "thank you" for loyal and repeat business.
2. Loyal customers earn the right to receive a valid reward. If they weren't enrolled in your program, they may have taken their business elsewhere.
3. Customers can see through transparent rewards.

The 8th ESSENTIAL STEP to Build a Successful Customer Loyalty Strategy is to MOTIVATE BEHAVIOR TO BENEFIT CUSTOMER RELATIONS AND YOUR PROFIT MARGIN.

In my experience, I find that many companies like the sexiness of initiating a loyalty program, but when it comes down to selecting the promotions and rewards offered they are not always as appealing as they should be. It's crucial that you select rewards that are relevant and meaningful to your customer base.

If you stick to the formula and believe in the concept, there should not be any hesitation about offering valuable rewards to your best and most profitable customers.

Hey Rocco, let me make a deal wich' you . . . buy this fancy car today and I'll trow in all four tires for free!

Ah, gee wiz, thanks.

This is *truly* where the rubber meets the road with ANY loyalty program and why it is so important for the rewards to be legitimate. For example, if you set up a promotion in which the cardholder receives one free widget after purchasing ten, you can't skimp on the "type" of free widget you offer. It has to be the exact widget you promote. The free widget you're promoting is the reason your customers will be motivated to purchase the first ten widgets to begin with.

The bottom line is this: If you want to be in the loyalty game, you have to offer attractive redemption items that are achievable for your customers to earn. If customers are willing to change their purchasing behavior and provide you with their loyalty, they will expect the same in return from you in the form of a relevant reward.

It's the Little Things That Matter Most

If you put on your consumer hat, you'll understand that it's the little things that matter most. As you strategize about differentiating your business, find a niche that lends itself to offering relevant rewards. One component you should incorporate is providing "feel-good loyalty." *Feel-good loyalty* is providing some type of offering that the customer will feel good about. Feel-good loyalty should be part of your overall strategy and will require some clever and creative thinking. Some companies offer free wi-fi, others offer free shipping. Whatever you decide, brainstorm hard, even hold an internal employee contest, but find your niche and add it to the mix.

Photofiddle.com is an internet company that offers a service to turn your photographs into art. Simply upload a photo, and you can instantly transform that image into pop art, impasto, a black and white sketch, and more. Once you create your personal masterpiece, you then have many options for the type of surface the image is printed on (glossy photo paper, canvas, etc.). Finally, you can choose from a number of print sizes and framing choices.

Although Photofiddle doesn't have a recognizable rewards program, it does provide various levels of feel-good loyalty. You'll typically receive your order in three to five days, and upon opening your artwork, each piece is carefully packaged and accompanied by a pair of white cotton gloves. That's right, white cotton gloves.

The label attached to the gloves reads, "All fine artwork should be handled with care: Please use white cotton gloves. Oils from your hands and fingers can leave fingerprints. Jewelry on your fingers and wrist can leave markings."

That's a personal touch, and that's feel-good loyalty. It's doing the little things that matter most to customers. It's thinking outside the box so your brand motivates your customers and resonates in their mind. Providing the white cotton gloves with each order sends a literal message and subliminal message. Photofiddle reinforces the need to treat your artwork with care AND the idea that it treats all of its customers with care—so much so that it even provides the white cotton gloves.

How can I motivate my customers if I own a hair salon and I only see the average client every three months?

Answer: Two words: challenge and opportunity.

It is no doubt a challenge when you only see your customers every three months, but it is also an opportunity to find a way to make something happen during the lag time.

In order to maintain contact with your customers during downtime, capture a cell phone number or an e-mail address from all of your clients. Create a monthly e-zine, or send periodic e-mail updates providing beneficial information that might be useful to your clients, that is, how to promote healthy hair. In addition, try to create an opportunity to sell new hair products or offer a gift card to your clients for every referral. You can even initiate a contest for a free makeover. Again, be creative in your thinking, and you'll be able to motivate behavior.

Is Discounting a Form of Loyalty?

Although it's not relevant to every industry, discounting takes place across many, and it is a big part of loyalty strategies. Retail is the obvious industry where discounting is most prevalent. Grocery stores, drug stores, convenience stores, and big box stores are characteristically heavy discount businesses. Many offer discounts, but only if the customer presents her loyalty card. It's a way of engaging the customer in the program and being able to identify, track, and motivate behavior.

I am a believer in discounting, but only as a single component of the strategy. I don't believe discounting should be the overwhelming strategy itself. You can motivate with discounts, but it shouldn't be the only motivating factor. There are exceptions. For instance, if I say GEICO, your natural response will most likely be: "Discount Insurance." Why? Because GEICO promotes "How Much Could You Save?" or "Fifteen Minutes Could Save You Fifteen Percent or More on Car Insurance" in every advertisement. For GEICO, discounting *is* its loyalty strategy. Remember, discounting can motivate, but be cautious not to let it dominate!

Issuing Points as the Currency, and the Motivator

Issuing points as a currency is a reward in itself. Points are an optimal loyalty program currency if you are looking for flexibility. By design, points-based programs are not as straightforward as cash-back programs. There isn't a flat percentage or cash-back amount designated as the reward. Points programs add a level of complexity that affords program owners the ability to be more creative in their strategy. Point currency also prevents participants from doing a simple calculation to evaluate the reward.

Issuing your own points currency is a differentiating factor in setting your company apart from your competition. None of your competitors will be able to offer their customers *your* point currency. That has value, and each time your customers earn points, they'll perceive earning the points themselves as a reward. Picture that—your customers feeling that every time they shop or take an action that you deem worthy, they'll receive value in return. What a concept!

Once customers value the points being issued, they will be motivated to take certain actions, knowing there's something in it for them with every purchase they make. In time, you can offer bonus points for select products or brands to motivate behavior.

Test your own behavior. How often do you go to the grocery store and pick up items you did not set out for or didn't really need? I would guess quite often. At the checkout you may pick up a pack of gum, a magazine, or a candy bar. Walk down the aisles, and your cart may have ten or more items in it than you set out to get in the first place. Now what if there were signs next to select items as you walked down the aisle that read "BONUS POINT ITEM." If you understood the value of the point currency and knew you would be closer to your reward by buying items that offered "BONUS POINTS," you would more than likely start to look for and purchase those items first.

The Power of the Point

There is nothing more powerful in the world of loyalty than the power of the point. When it comes to motivating customer behavior, points are a very valuable commodity. Although cash is indeed king, utilizing points as a currency has tremendous consumer value as well as value to you as the program owner. For consumers, accumulating points is addictive, especially when attractive redemption options await them when they reach their earning goals.

Earning points for purchases is motivating in itself. Offering points for each dollar spent or for each transaction has immediate gratification. Although customers accumulate points to build their point bank, they feel the process of earning points with each purchase is also a reward. The more perceived value you can place on the point, the more your customer will want to earn those points.

The more valuable the point is perceived, the more your customers will want to silo purchases by participating in your program. Here's an example of how the value of the point can translate to increased visits and increased revenue and profit on a per-customer basis.

The average driver frequents three gas and convenience stores on a regular basis. The first station is convenient to enter on the way to work, the second is convenient to enter on the way home from work, and the third is a more convenient station typically visited on the weekend and/or closer to home. For discussion purposes, two of the stations are BP brand stations, and one is a Shell station.

Of the two BP stations, a different franchise owner operates each. Because the gas and convenience market is so competitive and segregated, the driver may not be aware or even care to know if the BP stations are at all connected.

BP station 1 decides to launch a loyalty program, and the driver subscribes. Over the course of several weeks, he realizes he is starting to accumulate points every time he buys gas or purchases items in the convenience store. He also starts to realize he is getting closer to being able to redeem his points for an attractive redemption item such as 25 cents off per gallon of gas.

The next week the driver pulls into BP station 2. As he fills his tank of gas, it suddenly hits him. Not only is he filling his tank without earning the points he receives from BP station 1, but it will now take him that much longer to reach his goal of 25 cents off per gallon.

His mental wheels start to turn and it all comes together. NOW he gets it. Why should he continue to go to BP station 2 or the Shell station if he is not receiving anything in return? What loyalty are those other two stores providing? In a word: NOTHING! Although BP station 2 may be more convenient on the way home from work, the driver will now adjust his behavior to fit his own best interests. Over time he'll notice that the purchases he makes outside of BP station 1 is not paying any return for him. He suddenly finds himself buying his coffee, newspaper, milk, and other items in BP station 1. Why? Because he's receiving points on every purchase, which in his mind equates to earning a reward, that is, eventual discounts off his fuel purchases.

Another benefit to operating a points program is that you control the value of the point. You also control the point exchange rate. There are obviously several options for setting the point value and exchange rate which you control.

I have a Visa Platinum Card through my local credit union, Empower. The card allows me to earn 1 point for every $1 spent. At the end of each year, I typically exchange my points for gift cards. For 5,000 points I am able to receive a $75 gift card at many national retailers.

The program provides cardholders 1.5 percent back in the form of gift cards:

$$75 \div 5,000 = .015 \text{ or } 1.5 \text{ percent}$$

As previously mentioned, typical loyalty programs offer the customer 1 to 3 percent back, so 1.5 percent falls within that range and is a decent return.

So why doesn't the credit union simply offer cash back? Because providing cash back as the reward is dollar for dollar. Providing points as the currency incorporates margin.

With my Platinum Visa example, the true amount back to the customer is actually less than 1.5 percent because of two reasons:

1. Breakage (expiration of points or points that are never redeemed)
2. The financial institution's negotiated pricing on the gift cards

The credit union may pay 85 or 90 basis points on every gift card dollar redeemed. If the reward is cash back, the actual cost for the cash is 100 percent. Points programs provide a level of cushion while still being able to maintain a rich and upstanding program for the customer.

Point Expiration

Expiration of points can be set at any term you deem appropriate for your line of business. Typically, points will expire after 12, 18, 24, or 36 months.

Should points expire? It really depends on your program goals and if you can afford not to have point expiration.

Chase recently introduced the Chase Sapphire℠ Credit Card. The slogan for the card is, "Rewards the way they were meant to be."

One of the main benefits the Chase Sapphire℠ Credit Card offers is that the points never expire. By offering that benefit alone, its customers will have a sense of comfort and confidence knowing that all of their purchases will contribute to building their point bank and that the points will never expire. This feature has tremendous residual value to the cardholder.

CHASE ◆
SAPPHIRE^{SM}

Chase Sapphire^{SM}
with Ultimate Rewards^{SM}

ABOUT THE PROGRAM: Unlimited Rewards. Exceptional Experiences. Fly any airline. Stay at any hotel. Shop for anything. Get cash back or Pay Yourself Back with a statement credit. Direct access to a specially trained expert service team 24 hours a day, seven days a week. Gather family for a privately catered dinner or learn the secrets of a professional sommelier. Take a private golf lesson with a pro or an underwater photography class.

- Points never expire.
- No limit on what you can earn
- No blackout dates.
- Unrestricted airline travel.
- Any reward. Anytime. Guaranteed.

WHAT I LIKE: Chase found a way to offer a credit card rewards program with all of the perks and no restrictions. This card is the real deal.

FOR MORE DETAILED INFORMATION VISIT:

chasesapphire.com

Issuing your own points currency is a differentiating factor in setting your company apart from your competition.

Discover® Card and others dominate the cash-back space. Here is an example of Discover's current cash-back offer listed on its website:

5 percent *Cashback Bonus* on categories that change.

Up to 1 percent unlimited *Cashback Bonus*
on all other purchases.

Each quarter, Discover offers *Cashback Bonus* for specific categories. For example, in January to March it'll offer 5 percent *Cashback* on airlines, hotels, car rentals, and cruises. From April to June the offer is for home and fashion. July to September is gas, hotels, and theme parks, and October to December is grocery stores, restaurants, and movies. Take notice that the categories selected are relevant and characteristic of high consumer spending for those periods. Discover is an industry leader for offering *Cashback*. If your interest lies in cash-back rewards, study the Discover model. It's a rich offering, but it's also best of breed.

Typical rewards programs bank 1 to 3 percent of total customer spending in the form of cash back or points as the base reward. This is your accrued liability of the program. As competition with rewards programs became fiercer, bonus incentives were born. As with the Discover example, the base reward, be it cash back or points, could not stand on its own. The offer to motivate consumer behavior has been elevated to Bonus Points or Bonus Cash Back.

In my experience, cash back will cost you more program liability as the reward currency. With cash back there is not any breakage because cash is cash, but for many consumers . . . CASH IS KING!

Get Your Vendors Involved

As discussed previously, attempt to obtain support from your vendors in order to help offset the cost of specific promotions to motivate new purchases. If your vendors see that they are moving more products by participating in the cost of the promotion, they will probably continue to support the cause and even request more frequent promotions.

Loyalty and rewards go hand-in-hand. Reward those customers who are most loyal, but treat all customers equally.

STEP 8

GOLDEN TIPS

1. Incentives motivate behavior.

2. Remember not to fool your customers. Provide genuine rewards.

3. Offer rewards that are relevant to your customers.

4. Discounts can motivate, but don't let them dominate.

5. Points are a powerful motivator.

6. Use historical data to your advantage when motivating customer behavior.

REWARD Customer Performance by Offering Attractive Redemption Options

Customers enrolled in your loyalty program are there for a reason. They want to go along for the ride and are willing to play by the rules you set up for your program. They have affinity toward your brand, are attracted to the rewards they can earn, and are willing to be identified, tracked, and marketed to. These are the customers you want to keep happy and want to keep as your most loyal customers forever!

Why are so many customers willing to participate in loyalty programs? Why are they willing to carry around another loyalty card in their wallet or key fob on their keychain? Customers participate because they want to be rewarded for their allegiance and for the investment they make by being loyal to your brand. They want to earn the gift card at the end of the year, they want the discount on fuel, they want the free airline ticket, they want the cash back, they want the free cup of coffee, and they want the iPod from the catalog.

Your loyalty strategy is essential to the success and growth of your business. Airlines, credit card issuers, and major retailers have all embraced their loyalty strategies. It is a major part of their acquisition and retention strategies, and successful loyalty programs are fueled by compelling and attractive redemption options or rewards. Object: Do X and get Y in return. Many companies have found that their rewards programs are so strong and so compelling that their entire business model is structured around their strategy.

Breaking Down the Reward

In its purist form, offering a reward is in essence a part of your overall advertising expense. It is simply the cost of doing business with your most loyal customers who act by making frequent, relevant, or profitable actions. Think of it this way. Providing a reward to your customers is no different than paying a real estate agent a percentage of the sale or a broker for getting you good tickets to the concert. In actuality, rewarding your customers is probably the least expensive way to *buy* their ongoing business in the form of a reward.

One of the statements I often hear from companies that are researching loyalty is: Why should I give something away for free if I would have had the business anyway?

That is shortsighted thinking and actually a quite arrogant statement. How do you *really* know you would have had the business anyway? How do you know if the customer would have bought from you? How do you know whether or not your competitor is offering an attractive promotion to lure your customers away? You don't. You can only control what you can do to keep your customers loyal and enthusiastic. Rewarding your customers' performance is a means of justifying the expense of their behavior. The more they spend, the more they frequent, the more they respond to promotions, and the more business they refer should directly correlate to the rewards they are able to achieve.

Customers as a whole want to be rewarded for their performance. If the rewards have high perceived value your customers will probably take action in trying to earn the reward.

It's apparent, isn't it? People want to be engaged in loyalty programs so that they are able to receive and attain benefits along the way. If you are a frequent traveler and fly on the same airline, rent from the same rental car company, and stay in the same hotels, you expect to receive benefits from each. Again, people buy where they like buying and spend where they like spending because of some attachment to that brand. If their reason for continued loyalty is the actual rewards program itself, it is all the more reason your customers will be looking for and counting on the reward.

Customers get hooked on loyalty programs for one reason and one reason alone: THE REWARD FACTOR!

The **9th ESSENTIAL STEP** to Build a Successful Customer Loyalty Strategy is to REWARD CUSTOMER PERFORMANCE BY OFFERING ATTRACTIVE REDEMPTION OPTIONS. You built the loyalty program, and your customers respond by subscribing, which validates its existence. Your customers set out to earn their rewards, and rightfully so, because they bought from you. They realized the more business they did with you the more they'd receive back in rewards.

Rewards Program Pioneers

Airline companies were pioneers of rewards programs. They found a way to master loyalty by enrolling and capturing as much of the frequent flyer market share as they could. Their initial offer: Fly as many miles as you can with the airline in order to earn a free airline ticket. Many programs started out by offering a free airline ticket by flying and accumulating 20,000 miles. These programs were a huge success in the early years, and many continue to thrive today. One of the risks however, is that many of the programs were too rich and became too expensive to maintain, especially when considering major increases in fuel prices and major cutbacks in the number of flights. Airlines began to impose heavy restrictions and made it difficult to book a flight using reward points without booking considerably in advance.

While many of the traditional airline rewards programs such as Delta SkyMiles® and United Mileage Plus® still exist, more competitive airline programs have emerged with no-frills carriers such as Southwest and JetBlue. These new age frequent flyer programs are more about rate of recurrence and total dollars spent than about the distance traveled.

In essence, they are saying fly with us all the time and we'll make sure you can achieve an attractive redemption item or "free ticket" on a more frequent basis, and without having to jump through any hoops to get there. Check out Southwest Rapid Rewards® and the JetBlue TrueBlue® programs.

Each industry has progressive marketers that aim to cater to the now generation. Consumers are demanding more. The *now-generation* is growing larger, getting older, and seeking a better overall experience. They want more—now. The redemption options you offer should be attractive, attainable, and appealing across all age groups.

Customers Want Transparency

Consumers are smart. One thing to avoid when setting your reward options is creating a front so that the rewards appear greater in value then they really are. As discussed in Essential Step 8, creating a façade rather than the real deal goes against the reason for implementing a loyalty strategy to begin with. The same goes for selecting attractive redemption options. Your customers need to feel confident they are receiving true reward value when they are ready to redeem.

With competition so fierce, connect with your customers and provide enough incentives so they *want* to continue to do business with you. Every company does this differently. For companies such as Zappos, their ongoing reward to their customers is offering free shipping all the time. If the customer is not satisfied with his order once it is received, he can send it back at no cost to them and have a full year to do so.

Others such as Chase have had to revamp their entire value proposition for their rewards program to remain on top of their competition. The marketing message for the new Chase Sapphire℠ Credit Card consists of: No point caps, no points expiration, no annual fee, any reward you want, and 10,000 bonus points to start.

Chase has created a bulletproof product. It is the ultimate credit card for the sophisticated reward enthusiast. Its **Ultimate Rewards** program provides cardholders with real-time online access to their account purchases. It offers travel without limits meaning if the seat is available on a flight with most major airlines, it's yours to take. There are no blackout dates. There is opportunity for bonus point earnings at participating online stores and a cash-back option if you so choose. Its biggest selling *point* (no pun intended) is its great shopping portal; customers can choose from millions of items for redemption in its rewards catalog.

Want some help putting together your redemption catalog? Go to thepowerofloyalty.com, enter "REDEMPTION" into the search box. I'll provide you with tips on how to put together your own *best-in-class* catalog.

How Do They Do It?

How is Chase able to offer such a vast selection of rewards for its cardholders? ANSWER: It has great leadership at the top, a veteran staff, and excellent vendors supplying it with the superlative offers you see. Believe me, it is not sourcing millions of merchandise items itself because that would prove counterproductive to its strategy. It relies on partners to source the best possible reward offers in the marketplace so Chase can have a *best-in-class* program.

Below are SIX reasons to reward your customers with attractive redemption options:

1. Your customers will feel good about participating.
2. Your customers will be eager to buy in order to get closer to their reward.
3. Your customers will see value with each purchase they make.
4. Your customers will tell others about how attractive it is to participate.
5. Your customers will very likely increase their frequency of visits.

AND

6. Once your customers receive their reward, it validates their entire buying experience.

Predictive Modeling

One of the important exercises in developing your strategy is constructing predictive modeling examples around your outstanding liability and redemption expectations. Your models will be your best estimate at predicting the probability of your redemption outcomes. You can adjust your models with actual redemption percentages as the program evolves. Models help you keep a foothold on the overall program liability, which is useful and needed as you account for program results.

Depending on the rewards currency you'll choose, keep track of all points issued, discounts given, random rewards, sweepstakes, free product or service, and cash back. Your predictive modeling should take into account all program liability.

When you build your models, ask yourself these SEVEN thought-provoking questions:

1. How will customers earn their redemption (on every transaction, select items only, etc.)?
2. What will be the average frequency of redemption?
3. Will your customers be redeeming for multiple items?
4. How easy will it be for your customers to redeem?
5. Will there be any expiration on the rewards currency?
6. Will there be ongoing awareness and marketing reminding customers about redemption?
7. Will customers redeem by going online, calling an 800 number, or automatically once the threshold is reached?

What Is Your Mission for Rewarding Customer Performance?

Most companies will respond by saying, to *Reduce Churn!* It's expensive to acquire new customers, and you know how hard you work to retain them. It is not an easy task, and rewarding customer performance through offering incentives, perks, and special benefits is a proven and effective way to limit churn.

What is the best way to reward your customers? Should you drive customers back to your business to redeem their reward or offer rewards from a catalog—or both?

Again, these decisions all come down to your strategic loyalty plan. Depending on your industry, you'll need to find a redemption formula that works for you. Credit card issuers have found that their customers prefer a rewards catalog or cash back while most retailers prefer to drive business back into their stores through gift cards or reward certificates.

You may choose to figure out your redemption options internally or hire an agency to assist you. Compare the costs of each option. Conduct a focus group with your customers to see what they say. Look to your employees and ask for their input. Compile all the information from your due diligence, and put your best offer in front of your customers to capture their attention right from the start.

Attractive Redemption Options

Be strategic and systematic about the options you choose to put forth. After talking to your customers behind the scenes and deciding on your strategy, be sure to include various reward levels unless you'll be offering a constant reward such as in-house gift cards or cash back.

Base Offers. Let your customers get a taste of a reward early on. You may want to offer an incentive upon enrollment or on the customer's first purchase as Chase does by offering 10,000 Bonus Points to start. The earlier you can show your customers they are valued, the better. Permit customers to earn low-level rewards quickly or let them opt to continue earning at the next level.

Mid-Tier Offers. Successful loyalty strategies incorporate redemption options that have high margins and high-perceived value. Carefully choose mid-tier redemption options that fit the bill. Fill in the gaps and round out your redemption offers with mid-tier rewards.

Wow Offers. Every strategy should include "Wow Offers" for top performers. The wow offer can be the free airline ticket, $1 off per gallon of gas, a big, screen TV, or tickets to the Super Bowl. Even though more than 99 percent of your customers won't earn the wow offer, the offer itself will add excitement to the program and give your customers something to strive for.

Wow Factor

Wow offers are vitally important to any program if your goal is to create the ultimate WOW FACTOR (ultimate reward) with your customers. Many companies talk about the *importance* of the WOW FACTOR, but many have difficulty implementing. Keep this in mind: As a rule of thumb, the WOW FACTOR you implement will most likely be attained by less than 1 percent of your loyal base of identifiable customers. This limits your risk while allowing you to send an important message to your entire customer base that the ultimate reward can be reached.

Successful loyalty strategies incorporate redemption options that have high margins and high-perceived value.

Choose Your Reward Options to Best Suit Your Strategy

Points. Issue points on every purchase. Although it is not a "redemption option" per se, the earning of points and accumulation of base points and bonus points are seen as rewards in themselves that can be redeemed for something of value at a later date.

Instant Discounts, Rebates, or Promotional Codes. Your customers will not complain if they receive instant savings when identifying themselves as part of your loyalty program or receive a price reduction if they provide a promotional code you send to them.

Cash Back. As discussed, there is no greater perceived value than cash back. The program may cost you more, but this may be the best fit for your customer base. As long as you clearly define the program rules for participation, the redemption itself is as clear as it gets. A buck is a buck.

Gift Cards. Gift cards are a well-received redemption item and are a perfect vehicle for driving traffic back. There is a certain level of "breakage" with gift cards, and redemption results can be measured at the customer level.

Partner Gift Cards. Based on volume, you can purchase noncompeting partner gift cards for less than face value while offering national name brands as an attractive reward.

Travel Vouchers. Because travel is often viewed as a high perceived reward, you can turn your customers' loyalty into air travel, a hotel stay, car rental, or even a cruise. Travel may be the "Wow" reward your customers are after.

Frequency Programs. If you are in the right business, frequency programs are a great way to provide low-level rewards at very little cost. Examples are a free cup of coffee, a free haircut, a free hour of service. If there is a way to introduce a frequency program as part of your attractive redemptions, it can go a long way.

Redemption Catalog. Offer a redemption catalog whereby your customers can exchange their accumulated points for items. Your catalog may contain in-house rewards and external items such as merchandise, travel, gift cards, and sporting event tickets. Visit air-miles.ca to view an industry-leading catalog.

It is always good to sprinkle in some ancillary reward opportunities such as providing random rewards, sweepstakes, contests, and experiential rewards. Initiate random rewards and contests to stimulate "surprise and delight" in an unexpected way. Offer ongoing sweepstakes with entry on every purchase. Post the winners of past sweeps to humanize the offering. Many customers feel experiential rewards are an exciting alternative and will be willing to exchange a greater number of points for an experience such as a meet-and-greet at a sporting event or concert.

It is in your company's best interest to have your attorney write out the program rules, details, and rewards options that are being offered. Each state has distinct laws that may or may not affect the way you present the redemption options to your customers.

Dick's Sporting Goods was founded in my hometown of Binghamton, New York, in 1948. What started out as a small bait and tackle shop became the number-one sporting goods retailer in America. Today, the company has over 400 locations in 40 states, and Dick's offers ScoreCard® Rewards to customers that enroll. The value proposition consists of *scoring points* on every purchase made. The customer earns one point for every $1 spent. Upon accumulating 300 points the customer automatically receives a $10 rewards certificate by mail.

ScoreCard® Rewards is a good example of a loyalty program with a solid value proposition that is easy for the customer to understand and participate in. Customers know that every time they use their card they are getting closer to their $10 reward. The program does, however, have the potential to be more engaging for the customer and more strategic for the company. Assuming that the company has a loyalty host that maintains historical transactions, Dick's can begin to offer more relevant promotions to customers based on past purchases. By targeting customers and sending relevant marketing communications to them (e-mail, SMS text, and receipt messages), it has the opportunity to motivate behavior for specific products, categories, or overall spending.

Then, it can take its program to the next level by offering bonus ScoreCard® points on specific products or SKUs. Manufacturers and suppliers can participate in offsetting the cost of the bonus points issued when they see an increase in purchases from customers who either never purchased their product or who bought expressly from a targeted loyalty promotion.

Staples Rewards

ABOUT THE PROGRAM: It's Staples goal to make it easy for you to do business with them—that's why they offer a FREE rewards program. They're there to help you save when you buy the essentials you use the most.

Rewards consist of 10% back in Staples Rewards on all ink and toner purchases, **10% back** in Staples Rewards on all case and ream paper purchases, and **10% back** in Staples Rewards on all Copy & Print purchases.

Monthly Rewards

Earn an unlimited 10% back on qualifying purchases when you earn at least $10 in rewards within a calendar quarter. Staples Rewards® are mailed monthly when the value of the Reward is at least $10.

Redeem your Rewards any way you'd like—online at staples.com®, over the phone, or in any Staples store by the expiration date.

WHAT I LIKE: Staples Rewards is a straightforward program that is easy to understand and the savings add up quickly. Staples made it easy for customers to enroll and redeem. Once you join, you'll quickly experience the benefits and likely say, "that was easy℠!"

FOR MORE DETAILED INFORMATION VISIT: Staples.com

Roger L. Brooks

I talked to my 15-year-old niece Gabriella (Gabby) recently to gain some insight as to how attractive redemption offers may or may not impact behavior of a typical teenager. To prepare Gabby for the conversation, I asked her to read the introduction and first chapter of this book. I also asked her to complete the exercise from Essential Step 1, and list ten products or brands she is most loyal to (next to mine).

Here are her results:

1. iPhone
2. Juicy Couture
3. Facebook.com
4. Discount Dance Supply
5. Abercrombie & Fitch
6. Coach
7. Ugg
8. 7 For All Mankind
9. Tiffany & Co.
10. True Religion Brand Jeans

Gabby didn't have strong feelings one way or the other about how she is treated when she wants to make a purchase. When I asked her how she would feel if she could earn some type of reward for her normal purchasing activity, her demeanor changed drastically. She said if Juicy or Abercrombie had a rewards program, she would be eager to sign up. She also said that being part of a program associated with the brands she likes would make her feel important and more attached to that brand. Gabby's thought process echoes the fact that no customer should be underestimated based on age, gender, socioeconomic status, or any other factor such as their dress code.

Like many teenagers, Gabby has access to mega information through her mobile phone and laptop computer. She also has access to cash and credit cards through her parents, as do many teenagers. Her purchases, however, could become more meaningful or simply thought through with more regard if she was able to add a reward to the equation.

As you ponder your attractive redemption options, remember to include offerings for a wide spectrum of potential loyal customers. Consider the most sophisticated customers you have as well as customers that may exhibit naiveté. Each unique customer offers opportunity and value to your business, and deserves the right to choose a reward relevant to her.

My daughter Alexis (8 years old) is already beginning to show signs of being a loyal customer. Where does her loyalty lie? McDonald's, Cold Stone Creamery, Claire's, Justice, American Girl, and oh yes, Disney World! Get ready; there are some 50 million customers from the ages of 5 to 16 getting ready to devote their loyalty.

MEN'S WEARHOUSE®

Men's Wearhouse
PERFECT FIT®

ABOUT THE PROGRAM: As part of the Perfect Fit program, earn a $50 rewards certificate for every $500 you spend at Men's Wearhouse. Once a member, you will receive free ground shipping for all online purchases. Provide your e-mail address and also receive advance notice of sales throughout the year.

WHAT I LIKE: This program is clean and simple, and recurring shoppers at Men's Wearhouse are earning 10 percent back in reward certificates for every $500 they spend. Your dollar goes a long way here. If you buy a nice Calvin Klein suit and a pair of shoes at regular price, you'll earn enough in rewards to receive a free shirt or a very nice tie. George Zimmer guarantees it!

FOR MORE DETAILED INFORMATION VISIT:

menswearhouse.com

STEP 9

GOLDEN TIPS

1. Customers have joined your program for a reason—they want to be rewarded!

2. **Competition is fierce.** Connect with your customers so they'll want to continue to buy from you.

3. Incorporate redemption options that have **high margins** and **high-perceived value**.

4. Provide **rewards** and **incentives** that customers can earn early on in the process.

5. Your redemption strategy should **fit well** with your customers and in your industry.

6. Be sure to include offers that have a **WOW** factor.

7. **Consider all age ranges** when selecting your redemption options.

MEASURE RESULTS: You Can't Manage What You Don't Measure

YOU CAN'T POSSIBLY MANAGE what you don't measure. This statement is as true as it gets. All of the previous steps are irrelevant if you are unable to measure the results. Being able to measure results of your promotional or marketing campaigns allows you to properly manage your loyalty strategy in a thorough and efficient way.

The 10th ESSENTIAL STEP to Build a Successful Customer Loyalty Strategy is to MEASURE RESULTS: YOU CAN'T MANAGE WHAT YOU DON'T MEASURE.

Measuring the results of each loyalty campaign IS ESSENTIAL to the overall SUCCESS of your LOYALTY STRATEGY.

Because loyalty strategies are considered the new age of marketing, they should specifically accommodate the need to measure results in near or absolute real time. What does that mean? If you run a report on Wednesday and want to send a promotional e-mail to a specific customer segment on Thursday for a promotion to start on Saturday, you should be able to do so—no questions asked. Assuming you put the proper systems in place, the data you gather should be available at your fingertips. If you use your data to the best of your abilities, you will win in the loyalty game. The game I am referring to is not a potato sack or three-legged race. It is the game all businesses are in to retain loyal customers in the face of competition. It is the game of being first to market or best in class, and in some cases it is survival of the *quickest*: the quickest to be able to react, respond, answer, counter, or conquer the goal at hand.

Here are FIVE reasons why crunching your data in an efficient manner will keep you on top of your strategy AND your competition:

1. It will keep you reacting quickly.
2. It will keep you well organized.
3. It will keep you disciplined.
4. It will keep you proficient.
5. It will keep you capable of delivering relevant and measurable campaigns.

THE
LOYALTY
CYCLE
NEVER
ENDS.

Mining Data, Crunching Data, Massaging Data

However you term it, your data is the lifeblood of keeping your program fresh and alive. It is utilizing and processing your data within your loyalty host that will keep you a step ahead of your competition. Measuring the results of each promotion is simply essential in your quest to triumph in your loyalty strategy. It is the final turn you'll take in completing the next-generation loyalty cycle before starting the process all over again. The loyalty cycle never ends.

The first loyalty campaign you'll measure may be the success of your customer enrollment strategy. In theory, your loyalty plan should include your enrollment projections, which can be compared and measured against your exact enrollment activity. The numbers should be closely monitored by your program manager, and each person responsible for his piece of enrollment should be made accountable and kept abreast of actual enrollment activity on an ongoing basis.

It is vital that roles and responsibilities of each participating party be clearly defined prior to the launch of your program. That means everything from designing your enrollment forms to printing any collateral material should be coordinated in advance. Systems can also be set up so that each party contributing to the overall success of the program has an investment in ensuring the success of continued enrollment.

For example, if you run a chain of grocery stores, your organizational chart specific to enrollment of your loyalty strategy may look like this:

Organizational Hierarchy

- Register clerks
- Customer service counter associates
- Assistant managers
- Store manager
- Regional manager
- Loyalty program owner (corporate)

If each person in your organizational hierarchy is part of your enrollment strategy, you may want to consider putting in place an internal incentive plan or competition to create excitement and awareness around the success of the enrollment campaign. Employees in the chain should be rewarded for the success of their specific piece. The register clerks and customer service counter associates should be rewarded individually for each enrollment form they submit, while assistant managers and store managers are rewarded for overall store performance. The regional managers and loyalty program owner should be rewarded on the overall success of enrollment. With each layer in the chain holding accountability, the success rate of your enrollment campaign will increase.

Should you exceed your projections or fall short, the enrollment strategy can be modified to adjust as need be midstream. Changes or adjustments can be made while the enrollment campaign is in progress, which will save you time and money. Measuring and quantifying the success of enrollment is a good example of the need to be organized and structured for each piece of your loyalty promotion puzzle, which is unique to your business.

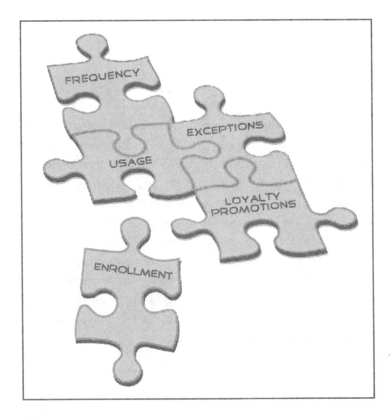

Your loyalty strategy should evolve and continue to evolve over time. There should be constant measurement of each loyalty campaign. The success of one campaign or promotion can trigger a domino effect that improves each future campaign. And you will learn to modify campaigns based on the success or failure you are able to measure.

Whoever you assign to having ownership of your loyalty strategy will welcome the opportunity to measure the results on a loyalty campaign level. Once *The Power of Loyalty* sets in, your program manager will not know how the company survived without it. When the program manager witnesses firsthand that an e-mail campaign or a receipt campaign sent to a control group triggers incremental sales, there will be nothing more exciting.

A few years back, I ran a loyalty campaign with a client who wanted to increase the number of e-mail addresses in the company's rewards program system. The client found that marketing to customers through e-mail was much more cost-effective and efficient than sending direct mail. A promotion was set up in the system with the following logic:

- Any customer who presented her loyalty card without a valid e-mail address in her loyalty profile would receive a message on the receipt which read: Receive 300 bonus points for submitting a valid e-mail address.

- The customer had to opt-in to receiving e-mail marketing messages as part of the initial enrollment process for authorizing e-mail communications of such promotions. After running the promotion for three months, the company increased its valid e-mail addresses in the system by nearly 20 percent. The point is you can design loyalty program campaigns or promotions around virtually any opportunity you see. The possibilities are endless.

I began Essential Step 1 by telling you it's really not that complicated and that what you'll read in this book is not astrophysics . . . and it isn't. **Initiating loyalty is taking what you already know best, putting some very proven strategies around it, and measuring the success every step of the way.**

Over time, you'll be convinced that there is not a more strategic or proven way to measure success or account for a true ROI than incorporating your company's goals and initiatives through your loyalty strategy. Although you may not see it as your be-all and end-all, it may become the most important tool you've ever come to rely upon.

STEP 10

GOLDEN TIPS

1. **Data gathering** should be at your fingertips and will be if the proper loyalty system is in place.

2. Be sure to **measure** the results of each and every loyalty promotion.

3. Clearly **define the roles and responsibilities** of your team members prior to launching your program.

4. Get your **employees** involved early on as they will be your biggest advocates.

5. **Research** existing programs to help you define your loyalty strategy.

jetBlue
AIRWAYS®

JetBlue—TrueBlue

ABOUT THE PROGRAM: TrueBlue makes it easier for you to earn—and keep—your TrueBlue points. And using your points for Award Flights is easier too, because there are no blackout dates. You can use your points for any seat, any time (as long as there is an available seat and you have the points). Earning TrueBlue points is easy. Purchase a flight at jetblue.com and get up to 6 points per dollar spent. Points don't expire. Just fly JetBlue or use your JetBlue Card from American Express®—at least once within a 12 month period. Earn up to 8 TrueBlue points for every eligible dollar spent on jetblue.com—up to 6 points when you purchase a flight and an additional 2 points when you use your JetBlue Card.

In addition, the more points you accumulate within a 12-month period, the more bonus points you'll receive. Once you earn your first point in the new program, your 12-month period will begin. You will have 12 months to reach these Go Big Bonuses.

WHAT I LIKE: JetBlue continues to thrive in providing excellent customer loyalty. In addition to providing everyday perks such as additional legroom, satellite television for every seat, and more snacks they have removed restrictions such as blackout dates.

FOR MORE DETAILED INFORMATION VISIT: jetblue.com/trueblue

Initiating **YOUR** Loyalty Strategy

YOU NOW UNDERSTAND the basics. You're ready to master the art of loyalty *your* way. Remember there is no right way or wrong way. Your strategy may look completely ridiculous to your competitor but be the right strategy for you. You are in control of your business, and you are now in control of your loyalty strategy. Take bits and pieces from Starbucks, Nordstrom, Chase, JetBlue, and Zappos and build a strategy that is right for **YOU**. Use the essential steps found in this book as a guide, and add your own flavor to create an appealing program that fits within your framework.

By understanding the fundamentals, you know that initiating your loyalty strategy is much more than printing up loyalty cards with your logo. Your strategy requires focus, determination, and heart. You also understand that mastering the art of loyalty is a direct result of the effort you put forth in learning what motivates customer behavior. The uniqueness of your business will echo the uniqueness of your loyalty strategy. Your strategy *should be* unique, and your customers will find value in the effort you put forth shown through the face of your loyalty program.

Loyalty is NOT a single and narrow strategy; it is a multitude of promotions and campaigns that make up your complete loyalty strategy.

Here are SIX tips for implementing your own loyalty strategy:

1. **Believe in Your Strategy!**

   Initiating loyalty is not easy, so don't let anyone lead you to believe it is. You must, however, be a strong believer and your own advocate in knowing that your strategy is right for your company.

2. **Find Your Internal Champion.**

   Every loyalty program needs an internal champion to lead the charge. Find your champion, and empower your champion. Who knows, maybe you'll be your own champion!

3. **Select Good Partners.**

   Be sure to carefully choose your loyalty program partners because loyalty is a long-term strategy. Select partners that will be supportive of your program financially or helpful in other strategic ways. Once you are ready, go to your manufacturers, vendors, and suppliers, all of which you have been loyal to over the years, and ask them to help support your program. Put a variety of sponsorship packages together and let them choose what package is best suited for them. Before you know it, they'll be knocking on your door begging to be involved.

4. **Choose Attractive Redemption Options.**

   If the redemption offers are not attractive to your customers, you are doing a disservice to the program. Choose redemption options that will appeal to a wide range of customers.

5. **Map Out Your Plan.**

   Map out your loyalty program plan. Create your own internal road map that will guide you and others in the right direction every step of the way.

6. **Set a Launch Date and Go for It!**

   Once your technology is in place and tested, your marketing collateral is complete, your website is fresh and up to date, your enrollment forms and program identifier are in place, your partners are on board, you're NOW ready to go. Set a realistic launch date, and go to market with your EXCITING LOYALTY STRATEGY!

Crawl, Walk, Run—Loyalty

These industry buzzwords should resonate in your mind as you plan your strategy. If loyalty is new to your organization, there's no need to rush into things. Crawl before you walk, and walk before you run. This basic and simplistic approach may be the most sophisticated technique you'll adopt. There are numerous moving pieces, so keep it simple. If you must, you should err on the side of caution. It's better to be cautious than reckless.

No Program Is Perfect

Don't sweat it if every single piece of your loyalty plan isn't falling into place perfectly. Chances are there will be some bumps in the road that will discourage you from acting on your plan. Stay focused, find alternative options, and keep positive. There is ALWAYS a workaround when you are passionate about your plan.

You may be asking yourself, why in the world would any one person or any company want to take on such a project? You may feel comfortable, content, or complacent and not want to rock the boat. That is how many individuals think—especially in such tumultuous times. It is those with the passion, will, and desire to better their company and offer more to their customers that will get to the top. Face it, *The Power of Loyalty* is about breeding better customers and doing better by your customers. Have the courage, feel the confidence, believe in yourself and your business, and build something that you and your entire company can be proud of!

LOYALTY PROGRAMS BREED BETTER CUSTOMERS!

Below are SEVEN tips extracted from the word LOYALTY:

L Look internally to ensure your strategy is positioned for success.

O Open your contacts list of vendors, suppliers, and partners. Contact them to see how they'll support your initiative.

Y Yes, total company buy-in is a must. Obtain buy-in from the TOP.

A Align yourself with a loyalty platform provider that will support your goals and initiatives.

L Leverage the relationship with your point-of-sale manufacturer (or equivalent), and ask what loyalty solutions are available through your existing hardware.

T Take the necessary time to plan for employee training. Proper training will lead to long-term success.

Y Yesterday's marketing methods are obsolete for loyalty programs. A new age marketing mind-set is vital to the overall success of your loyalty strategy.

The beauty of initiating a loyalty program is that you can design the program based on your budget and business objectives. There are basic loyalty programs such as an electronic version of the "punch card," and there are elaborate loyalty programs that permit customers to accumulate points for every purchase made and have all types of bells and whistles. Many companies, of course, start out with basic functionality and increase program benefits over time.

So why provide incentives or rewards to begin with? The reason is simple and should constantly be repeated—to gain additional market share through repeat business and increase the profitability of your loyal customers' transactions.

The devil is in the details on how integrated, innovative, or inventive you want to be with your program. It's all about how badly you want to gain that market share and how hard you want to work at retaining your customer base. If you have one store or ten thousand, have a dog-walking service or manufacture Ferrari's, administering a customer loyalty program comes down to outsmarting and outthinking your competitors while catering to your customers' needs.

And Then There Is Zappos

There always has to be *one* in every crowd, *one* that sticks out like a sore thumb. Zappos is an exception, and truly *is* a diamond in the rough. Zappos defies all the odds. It does so many things well that its entire business model and the way it treats customers *is* its loyalty strategy. Very few companies have been able to pull it all together like Zappos.

It has no membership card. It has no points to accumulate. It has no rewards to offer. It has its loyalty strategy, and its strategy works.

Zappos is unique to begin with. It has an exceptional product, exceptional customer service, exceptional customer loyalty, and an exceptionally loyal following. Zappos delivers quality all the way around.

Zappos' CEO, Tony Hsieh, has built the next-generation loyalty empire. He is a marketing genius who took a basic idea (initially selling shoes online, now offering multiple products) and raised the bar for the way every company should conduct business. Hsieh strives to be better today than he was the day before. He raised the bar for how the company treats its employees. But, most of all, Hsieh raised the bar on the proper way to treat and cater to customers. Hsieh is a leader, pioneer, trailblazer, and role model for attaining the highest possible approval rating for customer satisfaction and loyalty.

Hsieh found a way to break up the monotony. Zappos makes everything about its company fun. Every employee Twitters, and employees are encouraged to share insights into their world with their followers.

If you're ever in Las Vegas and want a tour of its corporate office, give Zappos a call. A Zappos representative will come to pick you up at the airport and show you around. I did a Zappos tour in October

2009. The tour was insightful and eye-opening. The mood was so uplifting; it almost appeared to be an act. But it wasn't. How can so many employees, in every one of its departments, have such a positive, elevating, and high-spirited attitude? Why are there so many smiles as you take the tour? The reason is this: Zappos employees are passionate about their jobs, passionate about the products they sell, and passionate about customer loyalty. If they don't have the right skill set to express such traits, they simply won't get hired.

On the tour, I was told that all new employees are put through a grueling four-week training session to learn the ins and outs of each piece of the business. If you are hired to work in its corporate office in Henderson, Nevada, as a customer service representative, you are required to spend a week in the Lexington, Kentucky, fulfillment facility to fully understand the shipping process. When the training period is over, new hires are paid for the time they trained, plus they receive a $2,000 bonus to quit. Why? The company feels it is less expensive to pay a new employee to quit early on if they don't have the passion to be long term.

Go to thepowerofloyalty.com, and type "ZAPPOS VIDEO" in the search box. You can see video I took while on the tour.

I wrote a letter to Hsieh once. Within a couple of weeks I received a call back from one of his top executives responding to my request. I didn't receive a canned letter or an e-mail from the customer service center. Everything Zappos does, it makes personal.

I send many letters out to CEOs, marketing directors, and loyalty marketers. It's rare that I hear back from them on the first attempt, let alone within a couple weeks. If I don't follow up, my voice goes unheard. I believe that's the reason so many businesses struggle. They struggle because it all starts from the top. If the CEO doesn't make it a point to return calls, his employees will follow suit. If the CEO makes it a point to return calls and also makes it a point to tell all of his VPs to return calls, they in turn have their managers return calls. There is a trickle-down effect.

I reiterate: It's really not that complicated. Be aware. Open your eyes. Look around. Work hard. Don't be lazy. Have genuine concern for your company and your customers, and things will fall into place. You can't all do it like Tony Hsieh, but you can certainly strive to improve customer loyalty each day.

I believe Zappos' success has *everything* to do with the way it treats anyone who interacts with the company. *You* become the most important customer to Zappos at that moment. Learn from Zappos. Read articles on Zappos. Experience its website zappos.com. Treat yourself to a pair of shoes. You can learn from everything it does. It gets it, and now you get it . . . it's simply *The Power of Loyalty!*

ScoreCard® Rewards

ABOUT THE PROGRAM: ScoreCard is a proven credit and debit card rewards program that helps financial institutions build relationships and increases revenue while improving usage and retention.

Since 1992, ScoreCard has proved to be a very effective loyalty-marketing program. This program will differentiate your offering in an increasingly competitive marketplace and will help drive your bottom line.

Here is an example of what ScoreCard can do as your turnkey program:

Scoring of transactions, maintenance of earnings data, order placement to fulfillment vendor(s), online administrative website operation, redemption accounting, customer service inquiries, and online automated airline ticket booking.

ScoreCard offers brand name merchandise and travel awards that include a variety of airline tickets and cruises, experiential travel, online reservation/redemption for hotel, car rental, activities, and more!

WHAT I LIKE: Whether you're a small independent credit union or a large regional bank, the ScoreCard Rewards program is the ideal all-inclusive loyalty strategy. FIS handles all of the nuts and bolts of managing the details and even provides turnkey marketing materials to help you market the program to your customers.

FOR MORE DETAILED INFORMATION VISIT: fisglobal.com/loyalty

Roger L. Brooks

Index

"There's no 'instant' way to grow loyal customers. There is a slow-but-sure way . . . You don't grow loyalty in a day. You grow loyalty day-by-day."

—Jeffrey Gitomer